THE
JOB
HUNTER'S
HANDBOOK

THE JOB HUNTER'S HANDBOOK

An A-Z of Tried and Tested Tips

DAVID GREENWOOD

KOGAN
PAGE

United Kingdom telephone area codes are due to change on 16 April 1995. The new numbers are shown in this book.

First published in 1994

Reprinted 1995

Kogan Page Limited
120 Pentonville Road
London N1 9JN

© David Greenwood 1994

British Library Cataloguing in Publication Data

A CIP record for this book is available from the British Library.

ISBN 0 7494 1384 0

Printed and bound in Great Britain by Clays Ltd, St Ives plc

Acknowledgements

The Jobhunter's Handbook would not have seen light of day without the valuable support and encouragement of Carolyn Whitaker of London Independent Books Ltd. Particular thanks are also due to the young people of the Jersey Youth Training Initiative who unwittingly provided the motivation for this project through their energy and interest in employment issues. A special thank you is also due to Jersey's Careers Officer, Sally Longson, for technical support and advice well beyond that which could be reasonably expected of her. The qualifications chart on page 111 is based upon an illustration devised by Sally. It is reproduced here with her permission. The application form on page 12 is reproduced with the kind permission of Barclays Bank plc.

David Greenwood
June 1994

Abbreviations

A level	Advanced level (GCE)
AS level	Advanced Special level (GCE)
BTEC	Business and Technology Education Council
CAM	Communication, Advertising and Marketing Foundation
CCETSW	Central Council for Education and Training in Social Work
CQSW	Certificate of Qualification in Social Work
CSS	Certificate of Social Service
GCE	General Certificate of Education
GCSE	General Certificate of Secondary Education
GNVQ	General National Vocational Qualification
GSVQ	General Scottish Vocational Qualification
H grade	Higher grade (SCE)
HNC/HND	Higher National Certificate/Higher National Diploma
HTC	Higher Technical Certificate
NC/ND	National Certificate/National Diploma
NCVQ	National Council for Vocational Qualifications
NVQ	National Vocational Qualification
O level	Ordinary level (GCE)
SCE	Scottish Certificate of Education
SCOTVEC	Scottish Vocational Education Council
SNC/SND	Scottish National Certificate/Scottish National Diploma
SVQ	Scottish Vocational Qualification

Note: The Scottish equivalent of the GCSE is known by its full name – Standard grade (SCE).

Introduction

Gaining, losing or changing a job has an enormous impact on your life. Few other changes have such significance and the process is often rapid. You can apply for, and get a job within a day. But even if there are two or three weeks between applying for a job and discovering the outcome of your application, the chances are that you will have been required to go through a process which may include writing a letter of application, preparing a curriculum vitae, and perhaps filling in an application form. Within that short period, you may also have had a medical check, a selection test and an interview.

Successful jobhunters are not necessarily the best qualified for a given job, but they are the best candidates. Their applications are well prepared and appropriate and, at interview, they perform well. There may be countless others who could do the job better but, for a variety of reasons, these people often fail to be invited to attend an interview. Others, who are shortlisted, miss their opportunity through lack of appropriate preparation or technique. As in all things, success requires skill and knowledge. *The Job Hunter's Handbook* details every aspect of the jobhunting process. It explains how to apply for jobs and how to ensure that applications have maximum impact. In recognition of the fact that luck also has a part to play, it suggests ways of ensuring that the odds remain stacked in favour of the serious, knowledgeable jobhunter.

Anyone seeking employment, or advising jobhunters, needs access to a wide range of information. These needs are immediate – an application form must be completed today, a CV must be in the post tomorrow, and a phone call needs to be made within the hour. Advice must be instant, accurate, practical and easily accessible. For this reason there are no chapters in this book – just 138 alphabetically listed topics – offering vitally important information about jobhunting and the recruitment process. In this sense, *The Job Hunter's Handbook* has no beginning and no end. As a reader, you are encouraged to open the book and begin reading wherever you feel it will be most appropriate for you. Move backwards or forwards through the book as it suits you best. Read each section as the need arises or settle down with a cup of coffee and use the book to plan your own jobseeking strategy.

Some entries suggest where further information may be obtained. Words highlighted in **Bold** typeface suggest further entries in the book where related information may be found.

Legal or statutory requirements described in *The Job Hunter's Handbook* apply, in the main, to England, Scotland and Wales.

INTRODUCTION

Employment and equal opportunity legislation differs in the Irish Republic, the Channel Islands and the Isle of Man.

Throughout *The Job Hunter's Handbook*, the masculine pronoun has been used in preference to 'he/she' or 'they'. This stems from a desire to avoid ugly cumbersome language, and no discrimination, prejudice or bias is intended.

A

Ability

When you start looking for a job it is important to have a good idea of your abilities – those things you can do which might be of interest to a new employer. Begin by considering your previous experience of work. If you are straight out of school or college, think about part-time or holiday jobs you have undertaken. You might also think about any organised work-placement schemes you took part in. What regular tasks were you asked to undertake and what skills did those tasks require? An office worker, for example, may be able to operate a word processor, a computer, a fax machine, a photocopier and a paper trimmer. A successful kitchen fitter must be an accurate woodworker and would probably also need some ability in electrical and plumbing work.

Then, think about the wider aspects of your life. In work or out of work, have you ever been required to handle money or deal with customers or members of the public? Have you ever helped to organise a social or sporting event? Are you a member of any clubs or societies? Have you brought up a family or looked after young children? Have you ever helped someone through a difficult period or supported someone in a crisis? What does this tell you about your ability to handle people, to organise and manage situations, to think logically and to take decisions? How do you rate your abilities in these areas? Where do you think your strengths lie? Make a list of your abilities. You'll be surprised how many there are. Most of us have more skills and abilities than any school curriculum or job lets us develop.

Now, think how you could convince an employer of these strengths. What proof have you? Educational qualifications might help. A good grade in maths GCSE, for example, might indicate your ability to undertake technical jobs. English and maths are also useful to anyone wishing to work in an office. In addition, there is a wide range of college courses that lead to qualifications which show your ability in certain areas of work.

Your **references** are another way in which an employer can see evidence of your ability, so when you apply for a job, make sure that you talk with your referees and let them know as much about the job as possible.

You can also use your previous work experience to indicate your ability to do this new job. Make sure that you are able to talk about similarities and differences between the job you are applying for now and any previous work experience. If you feel that you have a wide experience of work but few educational qualifications, it might be worth exploring the possibility of gaining qualifications through the **accreditation of prior learning**.

Acceptance

At some point during an interview, usually at the end, you will probably be asked whether you would take the job if it were offered to you. Having spent so much time and effort trying to convince yourself and the interviewer that you are just what he is looking for, it may seem like a crazy question. 'Why on earth should he ask me that? What does he think I'm here for?', you may think. An interview is a two-way process, however, and so, by the end, both you and the interviewer will be changed people! He may have confirmed or changed his view about your suitability for the job and you may feel differently about it too. On that basis, it is reasonable for him to ask whether you are still interested in working in his organisation.

It leaves you with a problem. You may have discovered that the job isn't quite what you expected. Maybe you didn't realise that it involved weekend working, or perhaps the information sent with the application form didn't lay sufficient emphasis on certain aspects of the work. After all your effort it's very tempting to brush misgivings or nagging doubts aside. You want to be offered the job and you are aware that too much hesitation in answering could indicate a lack of commitment. There is no easy answer to the dilemma but 'forewarned is forearmed'. You know the question is likely to arise so try to find out all you can about the job before the interview. Background knowledge is the key. If you have done your homework there will be no nasty surprises during the interview.

If you decide to take the job, think about your security. An employer may offer you a job at the end of the interview or he may telephone you a few hours or days later. By all means accept his verbal offer but if you are already in a job, don't hand in your resignation until you have your new employer's offer in writing. Some employers will offer you a contract to sign, others will require a written reply from you. Play safe; don't give in your notice until you have something in writing.

2

Accreditation of prior learning

This is a way of obtaining qualifications for skills already acquired.

Some people prove their worth by attending a course of study and sitting an examination at the end. The examination certificate tells an employer that they have a certain level of knowledge or skill. APL, however, is a method by which you can gain credit for your competency in the workplace. With APL, the proven ability to do a job can count for as much as a certificate gained through an examination. Accreditation of prior learning can help you to gain an NVQ (**National Vocational Qualification**). NVQs apply to many areas of work and they can be obtained at different levels. For each type of work, there are set standards of competency which a person in that field should be able to achieve. You gain the qualification when you can prove that you can work to the required standard.

Alternatively, APL can serve as an entry qualification for further or higher education. Don't be fooled, though, gaining qualifications through APL is not an easy option.

Details of APL opportunities in your area can be found through local colleges of further education, adult education centres and libraries. Careers officers and Jobcentre staff should also be able to point you in the right direction. Having made contact you will probably be put in touch with a tutor who will take you through the APL process. At the beginning, you can expect to have a fairly detailed discussion with your tutor about your experience to date and your hopes for the future. Your tutor will not expect you to talk simply about your experience in previous jobs. In many cases valuable experience may have been gained through voluntary work. As the treasurer of the local fishing club or a mothers and toddlers' group, you may have experience of bookkeeping and budget handling. The voluntary work you did a few years ago in a charity shop may count towards qualifications in retailing. As a voluntary helper in the local youth club you may have developed counselling skills. Past experience as a union official or school governor could indicate that you have developed skills in management or negotiation.

Having identified your strengths, the tutor will want to discuss the direction in which you future career could go. This can be difficult if you are out of work and your confidence has taken a hammering but the earlier discussions should have boosted your self-assurance and enabled you to identify areas of work in which your present skills would be appreciated.

Once you have a sense of direction you can begin to identify the qualifications that would be most useful and you can establish a plan by which you can collect evidence of your ability.

Essentially, APL is about helping you to make a collection of material which will convince an assessor that you have already learned enough to be awarded an NVQ certificate. Your tutor is there to help and advise you how to collect and present your evidence. Examples of work that you have done in the past, statements from previous employers, details of previous employment or involvement with voluntary organisations can be collected in a portfolio and presented for assessment. APL can be time-consuming and the collection of evidence can sometimes be difficult but it offers a way forward to anyone concerned that their qualifications don't reflect their true capabilities.

APL opportunities are developing all the time. You can even use APL to gain exemption from certain aspects of study at degree level.

In many instances, APL will not provide you with an off-the-peg qualification. This is largely because human nature encourages us to look ahead rather than dwell on the past. We tend to aspire to 'better' jobs and new challenges rather than looking for the soft option, so people use APL alongside current study to achieve a new goal. In the office, for example, you may have had experience of filing and word processing but have never had to manage the petty cash system.

APL can give you credit for the skills which you have already acquired and further study will enable you to gain experience of petty cash handling. Put the two together and you are well on your way to obtaining those qualifications you need.

Further information
Get Qualifications for What You Know and Can Do: A Personal Guide to APL, Susan Simosko (Kogan Page, 1992)

Address

You need an address. There is no point in sending out letters of application for jobs, or telephoning companies to see if they require additional staff, if you don't have a place where you can be contacted easily. If you are about to leave college, or for any reason have no permanent address, try to make an arrangement with relatives or reliable friends to have your mail sent to them. Ask if they'll take phone messages for you as well. Whatever arrangement you make, it will be your responsibility to keep in contact and make sure that you pick up your mail and messages frequently. Jobs can be lost if friends cannot locate you and you don't bother to keep in touch with them.

Advancing technology

Think back over the last ten years or so. Items of high technology which were considered expensive luxuries are now commonplace in many homes. Personal computers, compact discs, word processors and video camcorders are now affordable for a large number of people, and further developments linking telephone, fax, photocopiers and computers are just around the corner. Technology is changing all our lives and if it isn't changing the way you do your job, the organisation you work for is probably set to go out of business!

Love it or hate it, getting a job and keeping it depends on your ability and willingness to cope with technological development. Survivors are those who enjoy the challenges that the accelerating rate of change will inevitably bring. As organisations adjust to the changes, as older, less flexible companies go to the wall, many of us will face periods of unemployment. Use that time constructively to update and realign your skills to changing circumstances. Ensure that while you are in employment your developing skills are being recognised and, above all, whenever you are interviewed make sure that you ask 'What training opportunities will there be?' See also **Computer literacy**.

Advertise yourself

Sometimes you need to make your own luck. Don't wait for a job to be advertised. Why not place an advertisement for a job yourself? There are two strategies open to you. Either you could aim to reach the maximum number of people within a given geographical area, in the hope that some of your readers will be in a position to consider offering you a job, or you could target your advertising to reach a more specific group of people over a wider geographical area.

EXPERIENCED ELECTRICIAN

22 years old, fully qualified, with six years' experience of domestic and site installation work, car driver with clean licence, seeks permanent position in Hampshire area. Available for immediate start, good references can be supplied.

Contact Sean Smith PO Box 123.

Much depends on the type of work you are hoping to obtain. If you have fairly general skills and are unwilling to leave your local area, it may be best to produce a general advertisement for publication in a local newspaper. Most areas have at least one regular 'bought' newspaper as well as a number of freesheets. An ad in the freesheet may be cheaper but is it read by potential employers? Is the local evening paper, published in town each evening, better for your needs than the weekly 'countywide' paper? If so, is one particular evening better for your kind of advertisement than another? Only you can decide which is best for your purposes. Phone each one to discover the size of their readership, the distribution area and the cost of advertising. From this information you should be able to gain an image of each newspaper's average reader. Which is most likely to offer you the type of work you seek?

Before dashing to the phone, however, remember that this strategy has a couple of weaknesses. Your ad will be read by a large number of people who cannot help you and the life of your advertisement will be limited. Today's newspaper is tomorrow's chip wrapper!

Magazines tend to be kept longer, and they are passed around much more. In effect, although sales are often fewer, readership can be greater. Take a look in any newsagents and you will be surprised at the number of magazines on offer, but this is just the tip of the iceberg. For every magazine you see on the shelves there are at least another three titles in circulation which you have probably never heard of. At the last count there were no fewer than 9432 periodicals published regularly in the UK. Many are trade publications written for those with interests in specific business activities. There is a magazine for almost every kind of business and occupation, from architects to zookeepers. Most carry advertisements and you can reach a much more specific type of reader by placing an advertisement in the right magazine.

Lists of magazine titles, advertising rates and contact addresses are published each month in *British Rate and Data*. It may be available in your public library. *Willings Press Guide* is an annual publication which may also be useful. It can be found in the reference section of most public libraries.

When you prepare your advertisement keep it clear and simple. Use full words rather than abbreviations. State your age, qualifications and past experience. Mention the type of work you seek, and give an indication of when you would be available to start. Finally, don't forget to include a contact address or telephone number. If you are worried about security, or if you wish to remain anonymous, you can arrange with the magazine to have a box number.

If you are unwilling to place an advertisement in the press, there is another option. You could design a simple advertisement on a plain sheet of A4 paper, photocopy it and use it to leaflet all the firms on a nearby industrial estate. Alternatively, you could drop it through the letterboxes of all the local companies who employ people with skills such as yours. Yellow Pages is a good starting point for deciding which companies should be on your list of targets.

Age

Age is always on your side if you play to your strengths rather than your weaknesses. When applying for a job young people can emphasise energy, strength and enthusiasm. As a young person, you can impress an employer by being bright, alert and keen to learn. More mature people can emphasise their reliability, patience, experience and wisdom. As a mature person you can impress an employer by offering stability, sound judgement and an ability to take a wider view. If you're between 30 and 40 years old you are doubly fortunate. You can argue that you are at the peak of your effectiveness – experienced but still youthful! These are all stereotypes, of course. In truth, there is no reason why a young person should be any brighter or an older person any more patient.

Recently employers seem to have rediscovered the value of having more mature people within their organisations. 'Ageism', an attitude which favoured the employment of younger people for no good reason, is on the wane. In an ideal world 'age' wouldn't be a consideration. The only factor which should matter is your suitability for the job. In the real world, however, some employers seem to have definite ideas about the ages of their ideal candidates.

If you are younger than an employer's preferred age for a job, try to discover the underlying reason for his attitude. Could it be that, in his eyes, an older person offers maturity and experience? If you suspect this to be the case, make sure that you point out the quality of experience and level of responsibility you have already enjoyed in your working life and stress your reliability and sound judgement. If he seems to be looking for a younger person, emphasise your continuing interest in and fascination with this type of work and show that you retain a lively interest in the work by mentioning training courses you have attended. You need to let him know about the personal strengths and wide experience which you could offer and allay any fears he may have regarding your commitment and energy.

Some employers think that people who have been with the same company or in the same job for a long time develop 'rigid', inflexible attitudes to the way a job should be done or the way an organisation should be managed. If your CV shows long experience with only one or two employers, be prepared to deal with this at interview. Study the job description carefully so that you can explain how your experience has prepared you to take on the range of duties and responsibilities in the job you are seeking.

Remember, people of all ages have attractive qualities so – play to your strengths.

A levels

A level GCEs continue to be the examinations traditionally taken at 18 years of age after two years of study in the sixth form at school or college. Usually, candidates sit two or three A level examinations and the subjects studied are often allied to traditional school subjects. For years A levels have been the young person's key to higher education or 'good' jobs. They are still the hoops through which countless people jump each year but among educationalists they are frequently criticised.

For those wishing to enter higher education they remain an obvious entry route. It is possible, for example, to gain access to an HND course with only one A level passed and one studied. Be careful, though; there is a common belief that A levels are important regardless of the subjects studied or the grades obtained. This is not the case. Three A level passes in art, history and economics, for example, would not be appropriate qualifications for anyone wishing to get into college to study for speech therapy or psychology.

If you are thinking about entering the world of work rather than continuing in full-time education, there may be more appropriate qualifications to strive for. Careers officers are best able to advise on the most appropriate entry qualifications for particular occupations and colleges of further education will list courses in your area. If you are unsure where you want to go next, the new GNVQs seem to offer the best of both worlds. They were developed as an 'equivalent' to A levels but you study work-related topics rather than traditional school subjects. GNVQs have been called 'vocational A levels'.

Answering advertisements

The minute you decide to answer a job advertisement you need to have your wits about you and move quickly. At this stage, you may be undecided about whether or not to apply. Your interest may be driven simply by curiosity but your initial contact can enhance or ruin your chances.

Study the advertisement carefully. What information is missing? If you decide to apply for the job, does the advertisement tell you the name of the company or its address? What is the closing date for applications? Are you expected to write a letter of application and send it with a **curriculum vitae**, or should you ask the company for a job description and an application form? Your first move should be to make a checklist of information you require.

Even if you are a regular telephone user it is worth spending a moment or so rehearsing what you intend to say when you call the company. Keep it simple and speak clearly.

'Hello! My name is John Smith. I'm phoning in response to your advertisement for a mechanic in today's *Evening News*.'

You may be asked for your name and address so that further details can be sent to you or you may be told to write a letter of application, but be prepared for the unexpected. A hard-pressed manager of a small company may invite you for an interview there and then. You'll need a paper and pencil to note down address, directions and time. When seeking a job, always have paper and pencil to hand and make sure you get hold of the first edition of the local newspaper. Many evening papers are distributed shorly after lunchtime. Some vacancies could be filled by the evening.

If you write to the company for further information, use unlined paper of reasonable quality, never a scrap torn from a notebook. Untidy handwriting and poor spelling will be noticed and remembered, so if your spelling is suspect ask someone to check it for you. Alternatively, take advantage of your local **jobclub** and produce your own word processed letter. Keep your letter short, simple and to the point. Identify yourself as a prospective candidate for the job advertised and include your name and address so that further details can be sent to you. Make sure you send an original letter – not a photocopy. You don't want to give the impression that you are applying for hundreds of jobs. An original letter tells the employer that you are specifically interested in the job advertised.

Anything will do

Young people eager to leave school often tell careers officers that they will take on any kind of job in their desperation to enter the world of work. They think they are showing a positive attitude by being prepared to take on any kind of available work. Discovering exactly what they would be best suited for can be difficult. Extracting information about skills, temperament, or hopes and aspirations can be like pulling teeth. Young people smile politely and avoid showing any kind of preference for a particular type of job, out of fear that they will, in some way, lose the chance of a job in another field should it arise. 'I don't mind really. Yes, I'd give that a go. Oh, I'll do anything' are stock phrases.

Adults too, if they've spent a long time trying to find a job or if they live in an area of high unemployment, can become so desperate that they will be prepared to take on almost any kind of work. The need to earn money and get out of the rut becomes so strong that they

9

will tackle anything. It's an understandable attitude and, on the face of it, it seems a positive view. Well, it's better than sitting at home worrying, and who knows, it may lead to something else. After all, everyone knows that it's easier to secure another job from a position of employment rather than unemployment.

But if you're in this position, be careful. Your desperation and willingness to please a potential employer can sometimes be your downfall. An employer wants to hire someone with a genuine aptitude for the particular kind of work he has to offer. He wants to appoint someone who is driven by an interest in this particular job rather than a simple desire to find work. Tell him how much you would enjoy the kind of work he has to offer. Tell him why you particularly want to work for his organisation, but don't give him the impression that you are so desperate for work that you will do anything – even if you are!

Application forms

You don't complete an application form to get a job – you complete an application form to get an interview!

Most companies, even small ones, insist that you complete an application form. They can take a long time to complete and the process can be frustrating because they never seem to ask the right questions. On the one hand, you are asked to supply details which seem to be completely irrelevant to the advertised job and yet, on the other hand, you are never asked to provide specific information which could prove to an employer that you are the person he is looking for.

Well, that might be so, but before jumping to conclusions let's look at what an application form is used for and then we'll see why so many companies use them. There are always lots of applicants for most advertised jobs. Many will have some of the knowledge and skill required but many more will not. Some applicants will have misunderstood the requirements of the job, others will lack experience, and some may not have the necessary qualifications. It would be a waste of time for a company to interview every candidate, especially when so many applications are clearly inappropriate. So the form is a type of filter, a means by which an employer can compare your experience and background with his ideas of what the perfect candidate should be. Careful study of 50 or 60 application forms can produce four or five individuals who appear to be worth interviewing.

On the front page, an application form requires your name, address and telephone number. It puts you in the frame and allows the company to contact you easily. Questions about age and marital status are also frequent front page items. If you are fortunate enough to be offered the job, it is a simple matter for the interviewer to photocopy this page and send it on to the wages and pensions department. Everything they need to know about you is contained on that single piece of paper so you can be assimilated into the payroll with a minimum of fuss. It is in your own interests to make sure that your first page information is accurate.

Some forms, especially those from government organisations, may ask detailed questions about you and your parents' country of origin. You may feel reluctant to complete such a 'racist' section of the form but the questions are there to ensure that the organisation is complying with equal opportunities legislation and with its own equal opportunities policy. Equal opportunity employers try to recruit the most appropriate person for the job irrespective of race, gender or religious belief. These organisations check their commitment to equal opportunities by comparing the 'mix' of people employed against a sample population – they ask the detailed questions to see if they're getting it right.

The form will also ask about your employment history. It gives an employer a brief overview of where you've been and what you've been doing. There are no rights and wrongs here. Too many previous jobs could indicate someone who doesn't easily settle, a person who soon becomes bored, or someone who has never stayed anywhere long enough to see a job through. Too few job moves could indicate someone without ambition or someone whose experience is too narrow. At this stage you don't know what the company is looking for. Perhaps they want someone with a wide experience of work in a variety of companies, or perhaps they would prefer someone with a good track record of development within a single organisation. You've no way of knowing for sure so – as in all things – honesty is the best policy.

Application forms usually ask about your educational record and any qualifications gained at school or college. Some jobs will demand a professional qualification or a certain level of academic achievement but, in many cases, the employer will be merely seeking to establish that you have the ability to cope with any training which you may be required to undertake while working for the company. In some instances, rates of pay are linked to educational qualifications, but don't be tempted to give yourself qualifications which you haven't earned. In many companies you could face instant dismissal for giving false information and, in any case, the company is looking for the most appropriate candidate, not necessarily the best educated.

Questions about **hobbies and interests** usually also feature on application forms. Employers are often keen to take on 'whole', fully developed individuals and how you spend your spare time can tell an employer a great deal about your personality. Take as much care over this part of the application form as any other.

Most forms devote space to 'Further Information'. Many people choose not to complete this section in the misguided belief that they have nothing of further value to add – so here is your chance to shine!

11

APPLICATION FORMS

APPLICATION FOR EMPLOYMENT

PLEASE COMPLETE THIS FORM IN YOUR OWN HANDWRITING

Full Time	Part Time

Please tick relevant box

SURNAME (Mr/Mrs/Miss/Ms) *(In Block Letters)*

FIRST NAME(S)

HOME ADDRESS

DO YOU NEED A WORK PERMIT TO TAKE UP EMPLOYMENT IN THE UK?

TELEPHONE NUMBER

NATIONAL INSURANCE NUMBER

DATE OF BIRTH

MARITAL STATUS

MAIDEN NAME *(To be used for school references only)*

Please complete each section of this form as fully and as carefully as possible. We shall use the information you provide to decide whether we can offer you an interview and if so, as a basis for discussion during interview.

EDUCATION — Secondary Schools and Colleges attended

NAME OF SCHOOL OR COLLEGE	CONTACT NAME	POSTAL ADDRESS	Dates (Month/Year) From	To

All Examinations taken (Please indicate also Examinations which you are sitting, or awaiting results)

G.C.S.E./'O' Level/C.S.E.	Month/Year	Grade	'A' Level	Month/Year	Grade	Any other qualifications	Month/Year	Result

SECRETARIAL QUALIFICATIONS If you are applying for a Copy/Audio/Typing position please complete the following:

Copy Typing W.P.M.	Audio Typing W.P.M.	Shorthand W.P.M.
Can you operate a Word Processor **YES/NO**	If **YES**, State type(s)	

DS380 (5/91)

12

This part of the application form asks you to provide information under various headings. **After each section there is a space provided for you to mention your experiences in:**

1. Dealing with other people.
2. Having to follow set procedures, completing forms, working accurately, working to deadlines.
3. Having to learn new skills.
4. Analysing information, organising your work.
5. Supervising other people.

EDUCATION

Please give details of any other education/training/qualifications, together with any experience during your education relevant to points 1 — 5 above·

PRESENT AND PAST EMPLOYMENT (including any Saturday, evening, or holiday jobs/work experience/YTS)

Dates (Month/Year) From To	Name and Address of Employer	Type of Work Duties and Responsibilities	Reason for Leaving/ final salary

Please give details of any experience during employment relevant to points 1 — 5 above.

SPARE TIME ACTIVITIES AND LEISURE INTERESTS — Please give details of activities/interests and any experiences related to points 1 — 5 above.

Have you any convictions for fraud or dishonesty, or have you ever been made bankrupt?   **YES/NO**

(This information is required to satisfy the Bank's obligations under the Financial Services Act)

APPLICATION FORMS

ADDITIONAL INFORMATION — The following questions give you an opportunity to provide further information about yourself in support of your application. Please consider the questions carefully and let us have any information you consider to be relevant to your past experience from School/College, Work, your home life and your activities/interests.
Any information you provide will help us to decide whether we can offer you an interview and if so may form the basis for discussion during interview.

1. Why are you interested in working with us and why do you think you would be suitable?

2. Please consider from any area of your life (ie school, home, work etc) what activities or types of work you enjoy doing most and which you enjoy doing least? Please give reasons why.

3. Think about school, work, leisure time etc. Please give an example of a tricky or difficult problem which you have had and indicate what you did to sort it out.

4. How do you go about persuading someone to your point of view, or to do something? Give an example.

continued

14

The Bank is an equal opportunity employer. All applications will receive equal treatment regardless of sex, race, marital status or disability. To help us ensure that our Policy is being carried out would you please indicate your ethnic origins by ticking the appropriate box. The categories used are those recommended by the Commission for Racial Equality. This information plays no part in selection. It is required only for monitoring purposes.

BLACK	WHITE
Afro-Caribbean origin....................................	European origin.......................................
African origin	*(including UK origin)*
Asian origin	Other: Please specify
Other: Please specify	

HEALTH DECLARATION

The following questions do not form part of the selection procedure. Medicals, if necessary, will only be held after interviews take place.

The Bank welcomes applications from disabled people.

Before answering these questions, please read carefully the declaration that follows them.

Delete YES or NO where appropriate leaving a clear answer to each question which should be considered carefully.

1. How much school/work time have you lost from illness/disability in the past two years?   WEEKS

2. Is your health poor to the extent that you are not able to participate in a normal social and business life?   YES/NO

3. Are you aware of any medical condition, disability or inherited disorder which may prevent you from fulfilling your contract of employment without reservation now or in the foreseeable future?   YES/NO

4. Do you have any disability in any of the following areas?
   Use of Limbs .... YES/NO   Impediment of vision (despite corrective lenses) .... YES/NO
   Writing .... YES/NO   Bending and Lifting .... YES/NO
   Speech............... YES/NO   Working in any particular environment .... YES/NO
   Hearing.............. YES/NO   Use of stairs and public transport .... YES/NO

5. Have you, during the past two years, used/required treatment or counselling for any form of chemical substance abuse (e.g. tranquilisers, solvents, alcohol, heroin or any illegal substance)?   YES/NO

6. Have you during the past five years been referred to any specialist either at a Hospital or privately for any investigation/treatment or on a follow up of any earlier such consultation etc?   YES/NO

7. Are you taking any form of prescribed medication on a continuous or regular basis? (Other than oral contraceptives or a course of antibiotics or antihistamines).   YES/NO

8. Are you registered as a disabled person?   YES/NO

9. Please give your doctor's name, address and telephone number:

Please give further details of any disability if you wish, attaching a separate sheet if necessary.

Declaration

I have read carefully the instructions and questions above and declare the statements I have given are true and that I have not knowingly withheld any material fact. I am prepared to submit to a medical examination by an independent Doctor instructed by the Bank. Should I accept employment with Barclays Bank PLC, I understand that it will be on the basis that the truthful completion of this form constitutes part of the terms of contract for my employment.

SIGNATURE OF APPLICANT   DATE

SIGNATURE OF PARENT/GUARDIAN   DATE
(If applicant is under age 18)

Have you ever previously made application to enter the service of this or any other Bank or any Company within the Barclays Group? YES/NO*

If YES, give date(s) and particulars

Initially, would you prefer this application to be dealt with by the Regional Office that covers your
   residential area
   a Central London Regional Office
   by either
   (tick one only)

Please return this application form to: (unless an alternative address is indicated here):
Recruitment Manager, BARCLAYS BANK PLC, Personnel Department, P.O. Box No. 256, Fleetway House
25 Farringdon Street, London EC4A 4LP

Please leave this area blank for official use.

APTITUDE

So far, no question on the form has asked you what specific reasons an employer might have for considering you. What do you want to tell him? Use this space to give concise reasons why you should be considered for the post. Look at the job description and think about your background, experience, skills and qualities. Convince him that you could do the job and then hint at the additional benefits he could obtain by employing you. Above all, be enthusiastic.

Remember that when you drop your application in the post-box, you are creating a major problem for someone who has the difficult task of reducing a pile of 50 or so forms to five or six strong candidates. Your application is the only weapon you have so give him no excuse for turning you down. Spelling mistakes, sloppy handwriting or untidy corrections are all nails in your coffin.

When you receive an application form, always read it thoroughly before starting to complete it. Photocopy it and use this as a draft or else answer all the questions in pencil and get someone to check your writing and spelling before putting pen to paper. If your handwriting is untidy ask someone to type the form for you. Most application forms are photocopied at some stage so always complete them in black ink. (See also **Handwriting**.)

Finally, go to the library or local printshop and take a photocopy of your completed form before sending it off. Most application forms ask for the same basic information so life becomes easier once you've completed one form and kept a copy!

Further information
How You Can Get That Job! Application Forms and Letters Made Easy, Rebecca Corfield (Kogan Page, 1992)

Aptitude

Natural ability, added to a genuine liking for the job, equals aptitude – a quality which employers rate highly. Required skills can be taught on the job and many employers prefer to train staff in their own approaches to tackling tasks. Such companies are more interested in your aptitude than your skills. They can train you to do things their way, provided you have natural ability and interest. Aptitude is the foundation upon which companies build their skilled staff. If someone has aptitude for a job, an employer can expect to encounter few problems in training them and bringing them up to speed.

Take a good look at that job description and try to envisage what may be required of you to do the job well.

• Do you need to be able to handle people?

- Does the job require an eye for detail?
- Does it require particular skill with your hands?
- Are problem-solving skills important?
- Would you need an ability to write well or understand numbers?
- Does it demand physical strength and stamina?
- Is an eye for line and colour more appropriate?

Often, you can show your aptitude for a job by telling an employer about your hobbies and interests. Voluntary, charitable or community work can illustrate an aptitude for working with people. An interest in DIY demonstrates ability with your hands, whereas an interest in puzzles, crosswords, history or archaeology can indicate someone who enjoys tackling and solving problems. Participation in sports may convince a potential employer of your physical strength and you can use an interest in art, photography or interior decorating to underline your graphical abilities.

If some of the tasks required of the successful candidate are allied to the sort of activities you enjoy in your free time, you should have little problem in convincing an employer of your aptitude and suitability for the post.

Further information
Test Your Own Aptitude, 2nd edition, Jim Barrett and Geoff Williams (Kogan Page, 1990)

Assertiveness

Finding a job can be a stressful and intimidating process. There may be times, in interviews, for example, when you need to stand your ground and explain why you hold a particular view. In negotiating your salary or your hours of work you may need to inform your potential employer what is, and what is not, possible for you. At times, too, you may need to explain why you would be unhappy carrying out a certain aspect of the job in the way described in the job description. Everyone has a limit to what they are prepared to do, and at times you have to explain to someone where you draw the line. Assertiveness training can help you to do this effectively and tactfully.

People handle stressful situations in different ways. Some prefer not to raise an issue in the hope that the problem may never arise. Others overreact and nervously or emotionally argue the toss in a fairly aggressive manner. Both approaches can be counterproductive.

The assertive approach has much to recommend it. A calm, quiet explanation of the issue, followed by a statement of your position, can clear the air and nip potential problems in the bud. Assertiveness can succeed where anger, indignation and bluster would fail. Assertiveness is about clear thinking and understanding the problem in your own mind, determining where you stand, and getting that message over in a calm, purposeful way. An assertive person engages his audience with his eyes. He uses his voice, his body language and the expression on his face to get the message across. Many adult education centres and colleges of further education run part-time courses in assertiveness training.

Further information
Assert Yourself: How to Do a Good Deal Better With Others, 2nd edition, Robert Sharpe (Kogan Page, 1989)

How to Develop Assertiveness, Sam R Lloyd (Kogan Page, 1988)

Background knowledge

Every salesperson knows that you should make an effort to get to know your customer. When it comes to seeking employment, you need to get to know the organisation where you are hoping to work. There is no substitute for good, solid background knowledge. Set yourself a series of questions about the organisation and try to find the answers.

- How big is it?
- How many people does it employ?
- What does it do?
- Does it operate on a local, national or international basis?
- If it provides goods or services how does it compare with competitors?
- Is this organisation thought to be better or worse than other companies?
- Does it offer a cheap, reliable product or a more expensive, sophisticated version?
- Who are its customers?
- What kind of 'public image' does it have?
- What can you discover about the organisation from its brochures and publicity?

You can ask these questions for any kind of organisation, from a multinational corporation to a a small back-street car repair shop or a school. In your letter of application you can use the information to explain why you want to work for this company rather than any other. At interview your knowledge of the company will impress the interviewer. He will know that you are a serious candidate and that you have taken trouble to prepare yourself. If, during the interview, you don't get a chance to show what you know, you can always throw something into the conversation at the end. 'I notice from your brochure that you can now respond to a customer request within 48 hours. Has this been difficult to achieve? Are there any plans to improve your response time even more?' With a little thought you can always find a way of letting a potential employer know that you have done your homework.

Obtaining background information may require visits to the local library. If you are unemployed travel can be an expensive item so plan your trip carefully. Libraries offer you free access to the local trades directories which may produce useful information. Sometimes you can gain extra value from your visit by brousing through trade magazines to bring yourself up to date with current topics of interest in the business.

Jobclubs and **Jobcentres** may have information about the company you are hoping to join. You can obtain background knowledge by reading an organisation's publicity material. Check out its advertising and try to discover what kind of people it wants to attract.

If you are applying for a job with a small local company take a walk around the neighbourhood and see what the clients are like. Mention your interest to your friends. If you know someone who works there they may be able to give you a view from the inside.

Basic skills

If you could be transported through time and space and suddenly found yourself living in a primitive society, you would have serious problems adapting and learning to survive. You'd be so busy learning how to make flint tools, and fish hooks from pieces of bone, that there would be little time for rest or pleasure. You'd be one of the hardest working members of the tribe, and yet you'd probably be the poorest. Your lack of skill would ensure that you stayed hungry – unless, of course, someone offered to teach you the basic skills for living.

In our society the basic skills you need to survive are more sophisticated. Without some skill in reading, writing and understanding numbers, life can be difficult.

You may know someone who deserves a good job and would find this book helpful, but who has never learned to read or use numbers effectively. If so, information and help in developing those basic skills are available through the Adult Literacy and Basic Skills Unit (ALBSU) or a local evening class centre. Most centres have trained tutors on hand who will help to raise the level of skill either through class work or individual tuition. The teaching material is specially prepared for adults so the courses are relevant and enjoyable. Many people who experience difficulty with basic skills try to get through life without drawing attention to their situation. Problems frequently arise when they are offered promotion at work. For years they may have got along without needing to read and write or use a calculator. Suddenly, in the new job, new skills are required. They often feel embarrassed and alone. A better grasp of basic skills can be the key to a bright future. Basic skills tutors are sympathetic and discreet.

Further information
The Adult Literacy and Basic Skills Unit, 7th Floor, Commonwealth House, 1–19 New Oxford Street, London WC1A 1NU; 0171-405 4017

Best candidate

Every organisation, large and small, is trying to recruit the best candidate it can find for every vacant job. Take two companies with a similar product and the more successful will be the one with the better trained, more highly motivated staff. People give an organisation its competitive edge. The smaller the company, the more important its people.

But what makes a candidate the 'best'? Is it schooling, A levels, a university degree, or is it more to do with accent, dress, image and a pleasant personality? Fortunately, none of these automatically guarantees you a job. Different jobs require different skills and personal traits. The best candidate is the person who most closely meets the requirements of a particular job.

Employers have a variety of methods for identifying their ideal candidate. One method is to write a 'person specification'. This involves looking at the job description and imagining that the job had been filled by the perfect candidate. Then they try to describe what that person would be like. What sort of background would he have? What school subjects would he have been good at? How many GCSEs would he have? Would he have a degree?

Next, they might think about experience. Would the ideal candidate be a school leaver who they could train, or does the job require experience? What kind of experience would be ideal? Should the candidate have gained previous experience in a similar occupation, or does this job call for someone with wider experience in several fields? How much experience would be required to do this job – one year, five years or none at all?

Now what about skills? Does this job require any specialist knowledge or skill? Would the ideal worker need to be good with figures, finance or languages? Should he be able to operate particular types of machinery – an articulated lorry or a fork-lift truck, perhaps? Does he need interpersonal skills? Will he be required to meet the general public or handle potentially difficult situations?

Employers will also want to think about temperament. Does the job require patience and a careful eye for detail, or would it suit someone who is happier taking a broader view? Is this a job for an aggressive go-getter, or would a calm negotiator be happier here? Would it suit someone who enjoys office work and hours, or will the duties require someone to be out and about at unusual times? Would it suit someone who prefers to work in a team or someone who is more comfortable taking responsibility for himself and making his own decisions?

Temperament is also important when employers take their existing staff team into consideration. The best candidate may be the one who can fit in with the minimum of fuss or disruption. At such times, the ability to get along with colleagues is more highly valued than qualifications.

Thinking about such things enables an employer to compare your application for the job against his ideal. So don't be put off if you hear that someone with much better qualifications has applied for the same job as you. Qualifications are important, but they are not the whole story and, in any case, an inappropriate qualification shouldn't count for much. A degree in archaeology, for example, won't help anyone applying for a job as a swimming instructor. Experience, temperament and appropriate qualifications count for more.

Finally, bear in mind that it is rare for an employer to find a candidate who meets his ideal in every respect, so the candidate who seems easiest to train is likely to be selected. Skill can often be taught but attitudes may be more difficult to change. At such times aptitude is the important factor.

Beware of get-rich-quick schemes

If you discovered a means of making a huge amount of money legally for very little effort what would you do? Would you share your secret with the world or would you sit back and quietly watch your bank balance grow? Judging by many advertisements in newspapers and magazines there are people who seem to have discovered the secret to effort-free income generation, and they are so generous that they are driven to share their secret with you – for a fee, of course!

Beware! Their effortless way of making money is probably through the stream of cheques and postal orders which they attract from gullible punters who respond to their advertisements. No one is going to advise you how to make your fortune by any means other than hard work. If, by chance, you manage to stumble on the secret formula for effortless income generation, keep it to yourself. Tell no one – except the author of *The Jobhunter's Handbook*!

Body language

Human beings are complex, sophisticated creatures. We operate at different levels simultaneously and although some of our spoken messages are clear and easily understood, our body language works almost at a subconscious level.

Sometimes our posture, or the way we use our hands, can tell more about us than the words we speak. When spoken words are contradicted by our body language, the message becomes disquieting. It creates a feeling of unease in the listener and it doesn't ring true. No wonder most of us learn never to take anything at face value.

In an **interview**, it is essential that the words you speak are supported by the messages your body sends out. Telling an interviewer that you are cool and able to handle stressful situations won't be believed if you are wringing your hands or biting your nails as you speak. You could also have problems convincing an interviewer that you are bright and alert if you lean back in your chair and put your hands behind your head. These are extreme examples, of course, but they illustrate how your body language can sometimes let you down. But if poor use of your body language can damage your chances of success, it stands to reason that careful attention to body language can greatly improve your ability to get your message across.

At interview sit slightly forward in the chair facing your interviewer and try to keep your back straight. Television newsreaders do this all the time. Rest your hands together in your lap. Make yourself comfortable so that you are able to hold the position for as long as you need to. Fidgeting and constantly changing your position on the chair can give an impression of nervousness. Sitting comfortably and facing your interviewers can make you appear calm and collected, even if you are not.

If you are being interviewed by several people, each one will wish to ask one or two questions. Turn slightly in your chair to face each new questioner. It confirms to each of them that you are listening carefully to what they have to say. When you give your answer, try to look at each interviewer as you speak. Eye contact with your audience reinforces your message, confirms your sincerity and engages their attention. Try to avoid staring at the ceiling or towards the distant horizon. It gives the impression that you are struggling for an answer or are not really interested. Use your hands occasionally to emphasise a particular point. A simple gesture with the hand can be more effective than constant hand movements which only distract your audience.

You can learn a great deal by simply watching other people and taking note of how you react to them. Occasionally too, you can have fun and experiment with your own body language by purposely using gestures which seem contradictory to the statements you make. Be careful, though; at this subconscious level you can provoke some extreme reactions!

Business and Technology Education Council

BTEC provides a wide range of programmes of study related to many occupational fields in England, Wales and Northern Ireland. (See **Scottish Vocational Education Council** for Scottish equivalent.) BTEC courses are run in schools, colleges of further education, universities, companies and training centres. People study for BTEC qualifications in a variety of ways: as full-time students, on day release, through open learning or distance learning packages, or as part-time evening class students.

BTEC qualifications are available in subjects such as: the built environment, business and finance, caring services, computing and information systems, design, distribution, engineering, home economics, horticulture, hotel and catering, information technology, land-based industries, leisure services, management, public administration and science.

BTEC also offers a range of levels at which various subjects can be studied.

- BTEC First Certificate/Diploma – students must be at least 16 years of age. No qualifications are required to begin such courses.
- BTEC GNVQ level 2 – students must be at least 16 years of age. No formal examination passes are required.
- BTEC National Certificate/Diploma – students should be at least 16 years of age and have already attained the BTEC first certificate or the equivalent of four C grade GCSEs or above.
- BTEC GNVQ level 3 – students should be at least 16 years of age. No formal qualifications are required. This is a two-year full-time course or longer if part-time study is involved.
- BTEC Higher National Certificate/Diploma – students should normally be 18 years of age or over and have already completed an appropriate BTEC national qualification or appropriate A levels. In some cases, there may be concessions for adults who do not possess such qualifications.
- BTEC Continuing Education Certificate/Diploma and modules – these courses are designed for people who already have experience of work. Entry requirements and length of study can vary according to individual need and aptitude. Students may be admitted to these courses on the basis of suitable experience and proven ability in the workplace rather than formal qualifications.

C

Career change

There comes a time in many people's lives when they have to consider a change in career. This is more fundamental than simply a job move. Changing your career means leaving behind the occupation you were trained for and tackling something completely new. The decision to change career may be brought about by frustration in your present employment. Something you enjoyed doing at 21 could become a bore if you are still doing it at 40. Changes in domestic circumstances are another major reason why a career change may be necessary. Within the family, the career development of one partner may force relocation to an area where the other partner's skills are unwanted or even irrelevant. Young children or ailing relatives sometimes require more attention than a busy, full-time job will allow.

Change may also be necessary as a result of economic or political factors which sweep away job opportunities which were available in the past. It isn't only coal miners who feel this cold wind of change. In recent years fishermen, steel workers, oil-rig staff, civil servants, opticians, bankers, teachers, the military and a whole army of office workers have been forced to consider alternative employment.

When exploring the possibility of a radical change in career, begin by taking a good look at yourself. During your life you will have picked up a good many skills. Some of them may be specific and highly technical – learned through previous employment – but others will be transferable, good for a wide variety of situations. In previous work you may have been responsible for supervising staff, handling money, dealing with the public, investigating complaints, training new staff, writing letters, or setting up schedules and time-tables. Out of work, your voluntary activities may have given you management, coaching, fund-raising or negotiating skills. Qualities are important too:

- What sort of person are you?
- What things are important to you?
- Do you like a regular office routine?

- Do you like change?
- Are you good at dealing with difficult people or are you better at handling paper or machinery?
- Are you methodical?
- How do you feel about standing up and making presentations?
- Do you like to see a job through to the end?
- Are you self-motivated?

Completing checklists such as the above will enable you to get a view of the type of work which may suit you best. At this stage, let your imagination have free rein. Later you can compare your qualifications with those required by the career which seems to interest you most. You may find that you need to update your qualifications, embark on a course of training or gain recognition for your skills through the **accreditation of prior learning**, but don't be daunted by this; a change in career is an exciting development and if you find the type of job which you enjoy, the training should be enjoyable too.

Alternatively, try dissecting your ideal job and identifying those elements of the work which particularly attract you. Could there be a similar job, at a lower level perhaps, which has a large proportion of the same elements? Maybe you can't become a primary school teacher but, having brought up a couple of children yourself, you may be an ideal candidate for a job as a school assistant working alongside teachers in a primary school. If the teaching and learning environment interests you, you could consider becoming a training officer in a small company or an instructor on a **Youth Training** project.

No matter whether your career change is a willing or a reluctant move, it will affect every aspect of your life and it requires careful thought.

Further information
The Mid-Career Action Guide, 2nd edition, Derek and Fred Kemp (Kogan Page, 1992)

The Daily Telegraph Guide to Changing Your Job After 35, 7th edition, Godfrey Golzen and Philip Plumbley (Kogan Page, 1993). Both are excellent books filled with practical help and advice on this subject.

More for women: *Portable Careers: How to Survive Your Partner's Relocation*, Linda R Greenbury (Kogan Page, 1992)

Career development loan

Sometimes the job that you want is just one or two steps ahead of you. You feel that you have the right attitude and temperament but there is an aspect of the work that you haven't been trained for. CDLs aim to provide assistance to people who want to undertake work-related training but are unable to raise sufficient funds to pay for it out of their own pockets.

Anyone can apply – you don't need to be unemployed or in receipt of any benefit. Loans can be used for any training which lasts between one week and a year. The training can take place at a college, a private school or you can study at home through a distance learning package. You can study full time or part time and, if your chosen course is longer than a year, you can use the loan to pay for up to 12 months of it.

CDLs are administered by three banks: Barclays, Clydesdale and the Co-operative. You apply for a CDL just like any other loan but you don't need to have an account with that bank to get one. You'll need to convince the manager that your ideas are sound and that you can achieve what you set out to do. The government believes that loans are better than grants because you have to pay loans back and therefore you'll do your homework carefully before committing yourself.

You can ask for any amount of money from £300 to £5000 to cover course fees, books, materials and, if necessary, living expenses, but you must find a minimum of 20 per cent yourself (£20 for every £100 borrowed).

The government pays the interest on the loan during the study period and for up to three months after the training ends. During this time you have what is known as a 'repayment holiday'. You don't start repaying until the training ends and, it is hoped, you're earning money – having found a job thanks to the new skills you've acquired.

Obviously there is a risk involved in taking out a CDL. You need to be fairly confident that your labour market research is accurate and that there are employers out there looking for people with the skills you intend to acquire. You also need to be confident that you will be able to pass the examinations to gain the qualification you want. See also **Grant-making trusts**.

Careers service

The careers service is currently undergoing a period of change in which it is to be taken out of the hands of local education authorities in order to operate more like a large number of local private companies. Each local careers service will be required to provide a range of vocational advice, guidance and information to young people for up to two years after they leave full-time education.

Careers officers are highly trained specialists who have a sound knowledge of the entry requirements for a wide range of occupations. They can also offer advice about training opportunities and the local employment scene. They don't work for schools, where teachers may try to convince you to stay on, they don't work for colleges which may try to recruit you to particular courses, and they don't work for commercial companies. In effect, their advice is valuable because it is neutral. When it comes to making decisions about your career choices and discovering training opportunities, careers officers provide an excellent service. You can obtain information about your local careers service from your public library, town hall or county hall, or local education authority.

Certificate of Secondary Education

These school examinations were developed in the mid- to late 1960s to run alongside the better known **General Certificate of Education**. A grade 1 CSE was considered to be equivalent to an O level GCE. If you have any grade 1s it may be worth mentioning that they are O level equivalents when you write your CV.

Checklists

Checklists are a simple and effective means of keeping you on line. If you have an **interview** in a week's time, spend five minutes writing down what you need to do between now and then. Think about any background knowledge you may need. How will you get it? Will it mean a visit to the library? When will you go? What about getting to the interview? Do you know where it is, or do you need to spend an afternoon finding the place? Which afternoon will that be?

Write down what you need to do and when you will do it, then cross off the jobs as you do them. Checklists get you to the interview ready to perform at your best. But checklists can be useful in other ways too. You can use them to boost your confidence by listing your skills, you can use them to compare good and bad aspects of a job or a training course or you can jot down questions which you think you may be asked at interview, noting ideal answers as you think of them. A checklist can help you to decide the best course of action or it can be a simple means of keeping you on schedule and on target.

Checklists can be as simple or as complicated as you want to make them. The finance manager of one large Channel Island organisation once reported that the most useful function on his £2500 computer was a simple checklist. You needn't spend so much. You can write a checklist on any scrap of paper, and you can slip it in your pocket and refer to it whenever you need to. He can't do that with his computer!

Childcare

If you are a parent, the arrangements you make for the care of your young children will be crucial to your success in getting and keeping a job. You will need to convince an employer that your childminding arrangements are sound and, for your own peace of mind, you will want to know that your child is happy and settled while you are at work.

Some people are able to rely on members of the family to look after children while they are at work but others have to explore the possibility of nurseries or paid childminders.

There is no statutory requirement on local councils to provide nursery places so the size and quality of provision can vary enormously depending on where you live. Details of council-run nurseries in your locality will be available from your local education authority. Private nurseries have to be registered with the local Social Services Department. Staff should be able to provide you with addresses of all privately owned nurseries in your neighbourhood.

Individuals advertising childminding services (not babysitting) must also be registered with the local authority Social Services Department so you should be able to obtain names and addresses of registered and approved childminders from here too. Try to visit several childminders before you make up your mind about the best one for you.

- Look at the premises. Are they clean?
- How do the childminders manage the behaviour of the children in their charge?
- What food do they offer?
- What sort of play provision is there?
- How many other children are being looked after?
- Which childminders arrange trips and outings?

Try to spend some time weighing up the advantages and disadvantages of each one. When you make your choice, remember that you are buying a service, so shop around until you find the one which suits you best.

Once you have made your decision it is important that both you and the childminder are clear about the nature of the agreement you are making. Sort out the fine detail now. You won't want to be constantly negotiating the arrangements when you child is happily settled and you are trying to create a good impression in your new job.

COMMISSION

The agreement you make should cover:

- the days of the week when your child will be cared for by the minder;
- the times of arrival and departure each day;
- the minding fee and how it is paid;
- the agreed amount of notice by both parties to terminate the arrangement;
- arrangements for absence through sickness and holidays;
- costs of nappies, food and outings.

Finally, before you start work, it is a good idea to spend some time ensuring that your child settles into the new arrangements easily. Give your childminder as much information as you can. Any dietary requirements or special words or habits your child may have should be written down so that the childminder can refer to them. Let the childminder know a little about yourself and your family so that she has familiar things to talk about. It helps her to establish a warm and easy relationship with your child. Try to arrange a few visits to the childminder before you leave your child there. On the first occasion go away only for a short while but make a point of saying goodbye so that your child knows what is happening. Let your child take a favourite toy or comforter with him. You must be fair to whoever is looking after your child and you must collect your child on time. Childminders and nursery staff need to get home too. Remember also that you must keep your child at home when he is ill or infectious.

Some parents worry that a childminder will in some way replace them. This is highly unlikely. Good childminders have a professional approach to caring and they will work with you to ensure that they complement rather than replace parental care.

Commission

Commission is pay based on a percentage of turnover or orders taken. It may be earned over and above your wages depending on the amount of income you generate for the organisation you work for. Insurance agents often earn commission based on the amount of insurance they manage to sell. Travelling salespeople and company representatives are also frequently paid commission according to the number of orders they take, and sales staff in shops often earn commission based on the value of their sales. It can have a dramatic effect on the amount of money you take home at the end of the week or month.

If you are good at your job, and if the company is a fair employer, you can do well. Some computer salespeople, for example, have been known to earn over £100,000 a year. In one well-publicised recent case, a bank managed to negotiate a 'salary plus compensation' deal to buy its way out of a 'commission-only' arrangement in which one of their agents was making in excess of £400,000 a year.

Some employers, however, expect you to sell a certain amount each week before you begin to earn commission. They set targets which are difficult to achieve and, in these cases, you'll find yourself earning a fairly basic wage. Some companies offer employment on a 'commission-only' basis. This means that there is no basic wage at all. What you earn is determined by what you sell. In a lean week you could come home with nothing. This is not the ideal arrangement for anyone new to the business. Commission-only arrangements are for the well-established salesperson who already has a range of excellent contacts and extensive product knowledge.

If you are thinking about working on a wage plus commission basis, check out the arrangements carefully. You'll need to be enterprising and fairly confident that you can achieve the targets which might be set for you. You will also need to be sure that you can handle a job which offers an irregular income. Even the best products sell better at certain times than others. When you're working on commission you have to be able to take the rough with the smooth. Check out the contract or the terms and conditions of the job carefully before taking the plunge.

Computer literacy

The whole thrust of the computer industry is to make computers and their software more 'user friendly'. As a result there is hardly any work activity which doesn't make use of them. Computers check your purchases in supermarkets and public houses, they are used to book your holidays, pay your wages, record your library books and issue parking tickets. Children use them without fear or hesitation and you ought to feel comfortable with them too. Courses for beginners are widely available in colleges. You can master the basics with a ten-week course, attending one evening a week.

The ability to use a computer is a skill which is attractive to many employers. Computers can also take much of the drudgery out of jobhunting. Word processors can help you to prepare a **letter of application** and a **curriculum vitae**. They can store your letters and CVs and print them for you whenever you want them. With a computer you can alter a sentence or a paragraph without needing to retype the whole document. It will also check your spelling by highlighting any unfamiliar words or words with spellings different from those contained in its dictionary. Some will offer advice about grammar and punctuation. Computers are getting easier to use all the time. Adult education centres and **jobclubs** can often offer help and

31

support in using them, and many colleges and jobclubs offer access to them if you are out of work and want to use a computer for your job applications. If you feel that computers are too difficult for you to use, take heart: you run a computer program every time you turn on your automatic washing machine or set the video recorder.

Correspondence colleges see *Distance learning*

Cost of working

Working costs money. You may need to buy clothes which you wouldn't normally wear. Transport to and from the job will eat into your salary, and nursery arrangements or out of school care for your children could also be an additional expense. You may lose government benefits through being employed and, for a while at least, it may seem that working calls for a lot of effort for very little reward. On the other hand, when you are at work you probably save on heating and lighting costs, tea and coffee may be free, and some companies offer cheap subsidised canteen food or give luncheon vouchers.

Fortunately, while everyone likes to earn a fair wage, money isn't the only driving force. For many people, work is about having a sense of identity and worth. They like to get out of the house and mix with other people. It is important for them that they are of value and that they have something to contribute. Having a job is also about being independent. Even with a low-paid job, things can improve. Your skills and your contribution may be recognised and so it is often easier to get the job you really want if you are already in employment. In this sense, therefore, a job with a low wage can be a better launch pad than no job at all. It may not seem like much at the start but it's the first rung on a ladder. Climbing ladders is always more exciting than staying on the ground.

Counselling

If you have a difficult decision to make, or feel that you might benefit from talking your ideas through with someone, you could explore the possibilities of counselling. Counsellors are trained to listen carefully. They help you to clarify your thoughts. The process of explaining your ideas or feelings to a counsellor can often help you to understand why you feel as you do, or why you have come to adopt a particular attitude towards something or someone. By carefully asking the right questions, a trained counsellor can help you to arrive at a decision, shed light on the issues surrounding a particular problem, or enable you to sort out what you must do to achieve your personal goals.

Counsellors are not advisers. They don't offer 'quick fixes' and they will usually refrain from telling you what to do. A counsellor is there to support you in making your own decisions. He won't make them for you. Schools, colleges and universities often have their own trained counsellors. If you have left full-time education, there is a wide range of counselling services available. The **careers service**, the **Jobcentre**, your local **jobclub** or the public library should be your first ports of call in order to gain further information about counselling opportunities in your locality.

Curriculum vitae or CV

This is a Latin term which means 'the course of your life'. Often it is referred to as a 'CV'. Essentially, it is an outline of your life to date, presented in a concise, easy-to-read form. A good CV will be simple, short (two pages are usually sufficient; you can always compress or highlight details as necessary) and clear but it will be enough to enable an employer to see that you have the skills and qualities to match the job advertised.

Everyone is unique. Your background, qualifications, skills and life experiences are different from those of anyone else and so your CV will be yours alone. Although each CV is unique, many are composed to a fairly standard format. They are usually divided into five or six sections.

General

Begin your standard CV by putting the title 'Curriculum Vitae' at the top of the page with a sub-title 'Personal Details' underneath. Put your name, address, telephone number, date of birth and nationality in this section and then, lower down, put a new sub-title 'Education'. This section of your CV should give the names of the schools and colleges you attended with dates and details of any qualifications you obtained there.

The next sub-title should be 'Employment'. Here you should list in reverse date order the various organisations you have worked for, the jobs you did and the dates of your employment. In this section too you could give details of particular responsibilities or achievements in each post.

Further down the page you could add a 'Training Record', listing the various courses and qualifications you have obtained since leaving full-time education. Some people prefer to include this information at the bottom of the page in a section sub-titled 'Additional Information'.

CURRICULUM VITAE

CURRICULUM VITAE

NAME	Judith Green	
ADDRESS	3 Park Road West Park Estate Leeds LE7 9NE	
TELEPHONE	0574 857923	
DATE OF BIRTH	29/6/1963	
NATIONALITY	British	
MARITAL STATUS	Single	

EDUCATION

Sept 1974– May 1979	Leeds Girls High Leeds	GCSE subjects and grades: English C, maths D, art C, general science D
Sept 1979– July 1980	Moorehouse College of Further Education	Typing, shorthand and office skills RSA grades 1 & 2

EMPLOYMENT

Jan 1987– Present day	Jones Bros Exporters Leeds	**Secretary to the Director** Providing a full range of secretarial services including the production of letters, contracts and reports, minuting meetings, management of appointments and making overseas travel arrangements
June 1983– Dec 1986	Excell Computers Ltd Leeds	**Word processor operator** Responsible for producing a wide range of docu- ments using a number of software packages including spreadsheets and DTP
Aug 1980– May 1983	Northern Printers Huddersfield	**Typist/Receptionist** Variety of administrative tasks

HOBBIES AND INTERESTS
Keep fit, badminton, swimming, travel, crosswords, collecting old post-cards, cats

ADDITIONAL INFORMATION
I believe I have enjoyed a successful career to date and at present I hold a very responsible position of trust within my company. I am hard working, trustworthy and although I enjoy working in a team, I can work alone without supervision. I am eager to advance my career and would welcome the opportunity of greater responsibility.

REFERENCES
Mr B McKinney
(Managing Director Jones Bros)
12–15 Scots Lane
Leeds LE2 7NE
0532 456789

Mr P Kitchen
(Accountant)
Excell Computers
27 Dales Rd
Moorvale
Leeds LE4 9NE
0532 987654

Most people also include a section sub-titled 'Hobbies and Interests'. This is the section which allows you to present yourself as a well-rounded individual with a life beyond the office or factory walls.

When you complete the 'Additional Information' section, try to make a few short statements which will be of interest to this particular employer. If you are applying for a job which involves driving, for example, say that you have a clean licence and state the categories of vehicle you are permitted to drive. Mention any qualities which you feel you have: 'I am punctual, reliable and able to work accurately under pressure.' The final section on many CVs is sub-titled 'References'; it gives the names, addresses and telephone numbers of two people who are prepared to give character references on you.

Young people often experience difficulty in compiling a CV. If you are about to leave school or college, you may feel that you have little to say. Well, it's true that you may not have had many full-time jobs, but you should be able to complete most other sections of the CV just like anyone else. In the employment section you can mention any Saturday or holiday jobs you have had, as well as any work-experience placements you have undertaken. When employers consider taking on a young person they don't expect them to have had a long experience of work. But a good reference from a work-experience placement and a record for reliability in a Saturday job can often count for a good deal, so don't sell yourself short. In the 'Additional Interests' section, mention any achievements at school or college. Did you take part in any fund-raising activities for charity or sporting events? Were you a member of any clubs or societies? Are you learning to drive?

Functional

People seeking high-level appointments sometimes prepare 'functional CVs'. Rather than simply listing previous jobs in chronological order, they are constructed to show how an individual's skills and responsibilities have developed to meet the requirements of the job they are seeking.

Begin a functional CV by giving your name, address and telephone number as with any other CV. Below, show how you meet the requirements of this job by giving details of yourself under headings such as 'Current Experience', 'Previous Experience', 'Achievements' and 'Qualifications'. On a second page, you can write out your employment and educational record like any other CV, but this will be much more condensed than you would expect to see in a more conventional CV because your relevant skills, experience and qualifications will already have been mentioned in the previous sections.

Functional CVs are sometimes referred to as 'achievement-oriented CVs'. They can be particularly useful if awkward gaps in your working life need to be accounted for or if you are trying to change the direction of your career. A functional CV allows you to highlight relevent experience which would not necessarily be obvious to anyone looking at your current or previous job titles. It also allows you to display it prominently on the front page of your CV.

In general, a CV is useful because it allows you to give an employer a great deal of basic information about yourself in an easy-to-read way. It may seem strange spending time compiling a CV when much of the information it contains could be put on an application form. Not every employer has an application form however, and, in any case, many interviewers find it easier to read about you from a well constructed CV than from a general application form which was probably designed years ago for many different types of job.

Without an application form, there is no alternative to preparing a good CV. You would have great difficulty putting all that information into a letter of application and managing to keep it simple and easy to read. With a CV enclosed in your application you can use your letter of application to enlarge on the basic information and explain why you want this particular job.

Putting together a good CV can be a laborious job. Preparing it

CURRICULUM VITAE

NAME   James White

ADDRESS   3 Castle Crescent
               Bardon Mill
               Nottingham N27 9MD

TELEPHONE 0685 968033

CURRENT WORK EXPERIENCE
Personnel manager responsible for recruitment, selection and development of over 700 staff within Compalex Systems Ltd, a large company manufacturing information technology components. While in this post I worked as a member of the senior management team and took responsibility for developing the organisation structure, identifying and recruiting key managers to support expansion into the European market.

PREVIOUS WORK
During the past ten years I have held senior personnel posts in two manufacturing organisations and the regional offices of a major high street bank. I am familiar with all aspects of human resource management including organisational review, pay and conditions negotiation, recruitment and the development of a wide range of staff at all levels.

QUALIFICATIONS
BSc Economics   University of Bristol 1972
Certificate in Personnel   Institute of Personnel
Practice   Management 1984

EDUCATION
Sept 1964– May 1969	St Thomas Aquinas Grammar, Leeds	**6 O level GCE passes:** English, maths, physics, chemistry, geography, history
Sept 1969– June 1972	Porterhouse College University of Bristol	**BSc Economics**

EMPLOYMENT
Jan 1991– present day	Compalex Systems Ltd Nottingham	**Personnel manager**

CURRICULUM VITAE

July 1985– Dec 1990	Speedwell Components Ltd, Thirsk	**Personnel manager**
Jan 1981– June 1985	Upminster Bank plc York	**Personnel officer**
June 1976– Dec 1980	Rose Computers Ltd Leeds	**Personnel officer**
Aug 1972– May 1976	Exon Services Newark, Nottinghamshire	**Training officer**

INTERESTS
Squash, travel, sailing

PERSONAL DETAILS:
DATE OF BIRTH   21/5/1953

NATIONALITY   British

MARITAL STATUS   Married

REFERENCES

Mr B Robertson	Mr P Kenney
(Managing Director)	(Manager)
Compalex Systems	Upminster Bank
192 St Nicholas St	23 New Street Rd
Nottingham MD2 9JD	York YK43 SD23
0602 111111	0904 222222

requires patience and a good deal of effort, but once you have your standard CV designed, it is a relatively simple matter to keep it up to date and relevant. Few changes will be required to produce a CV tailor-made to suit any job application you care to make. Your CV can be prepared on a personal computer and stored on your own disk. Many libraries, adult education centres and colleges of further education have CV building software packages available for use. You construct your own CV by simply following the instructions and answering the questions as they come on to the screen.

Further information
Preparing Your Own CV, Rebecca Corfield (Kogan Page, 1990)

D

Declaring convictions

If you have a criminal record and you are looking for a job, you need to know about the Rehabilitation of Offenders Act. The Act allows people with criminal records to have the slate wiped clean after a certain period.

When you are applying for a job, most criminal convictions do not have to be declared after a certain time; they are considered to be 'spent'. This is called the rehabilitation period, and its length is dependent on the offence and the sentence received.

People aged 17 or over when convicted, who are given a sentence of more than six months but less than two and a half years have a rehabilitation period of ten years. Those under 17 at the time of the conviction would be given a five-year rehabilitation period. Over 17-year-olds given prison sentences of six months or less would have rehabilitation periods of seven years and those under 17 at the time of conviction would have to wait three and a half years before they could state that they had no criminal record. There are shorter rehabilitation periods for offences which incur fines, community service orders, probation, supervision or care orders. The rehabilitation period is calculated from the date of conviction. After this period, in most cases, provided your sentence was not more than two and a half years, you do not need to tell an employer about it even if you are asked.

If you have a criminal record which is not yet spent, you have to declare it only if you are asked. However, it is always worth spending time thinking about how to tackle this question if it arises.

When you apply for a job you need to present yourself in the most positive way you can. The best way to handle questions about previous convictions is to give a clear, straightforward description of the offence with dates and a description of the sentence you received. Then reassure the interviewer by giving him good reasons why he shouldn't dwell too deeply on this aspect of your history. The factors which led you to commit the offence may no longer apply, perhaps it was a minor offence, a one-off incident or perhaps you were simply young and foolish. You may also be able to tell the interviewer that you have since developed a more positive side to your character.

When applying for a job, there are four occasions when you may be asked about previous convictions. Some **application forms** ask for details of criminal convictions. The best advice here is to write 'see letter enclosed', and give a short description of your offence in a letter to the employer. Include in your letter reasons why the employer shouldn't be put off by your record. Seal the letter in an envelope and mark it 'Confidential', for the attention of the manager or personnel officer responsible for recruiting to this post.

Application forms also usually ask you to describe your employment history. This can be difficult if you have spent time in prison. Here, you could write 'Unavailable for work', or 'Not in employment'. Once again, an enclosed 'Confidential' letter could be included. In this way, you ensure that the application form puts you in a positive light and that you have the chance to explain the situation fully in your enclosed letter.

At interview, an employer who doesn't know of your past may ask you about previous convictions. This is often a general question and some interviewers could be shocked by your unexpected disclosure. If you feel that the interview is the best place for you to disclose your convictions, it may be worth telling your interviewer that you have something of a personal nature to discuss with him. He won't know what it is but at least he'll be ready to discuss something slightly out of the ordinary. Before the interview rehearse what you intend to say and make sure that you promote the positive aspects of your life since the offence was committed.

Some people prefer not to disclose information until they are offered the job. This is a risky strategy. The employer will almost certainly be taken aback. If he makes the offer of employment subject to references, however, and you feel that his enquiries may lead him to discover your convictions, it is better that he hears the truth from you rather than anyone else. If you avoid telling him until you take up employment, his reaction could be unpredictable. He may feel cheated and look for ways of dismissing you. Declaring convictions at this stage carries a high level of risk. If you've come so far and he hasn't asked you about previous spent convictions it may be better not to raise the matter. After all, if he doesn't ask, you needn't tell him.

There are some jobs to which the Rehabilitation of Offenders Act does not apply. When applying for jobs which are excepted from the Act, you must declare all criminal convictions no matter how old they are. Your statement is often tested by a police check. Jobs which are excepted include:

- Those, paid or voluntary, in which there would be substantial access to people under the age of 18. Professions which have

legal protection such as lawyers, doctors, dentists, nurses and chemists.
- Jobs where national security may be at risk, such as some civil service posts, defence contractors and sensitive jobs within the BBC, British Telecom or the Post Office. Application forms for excepted posts are usually clearly marked.

Further information
The National Association for the Care and Resettlement of Offenders (NACRO), 169 Clapham Road, London SW9 0PU; 0171-582 6500

Straight for Work published by Next-Step Training Ltd, 12–18 Hoxton Street, London N1 5SG; 0171-729 5979. £2.90 including postage and packing

Depression

Normally, most people have a well-developed system for rewarding themselves. If they've had a busy time at work during the week, they might take a box of chocolates home for the weekend. Well, they've worked hard and so they've earned it. Other people manage to smile through all sorts of difficulties in their job because they know that none of it will matter on Saturday when they go to watch their team play, or on Sunday morning when they get the chance to try out a new fishing rod.

Some people 'reward' themselves by owning a good car, being a member of a club or planning long-haul holidays. Some simply look forward to a drive to the coast at the weekend or a walk in the countryside with the dog. For a few lucky individuals, the job they do is a reward in itself.

Depression is a state of mind which people get into when their reward system breaks down. Perhaps their job doesn't offer the level of satisfaction that it used to, or because they are out of work, they are unable to give themselves the rewards which they value. Either way, anyone trying to find a job, or change the one they've got, is vulnerable. A person's self-image can take a battering at this time and the damage can be reinforced by failing to get the first few jobs applied for.

There is no easy solution and even people who know what to expect can still suffer bouts of depression during periods of unemployment. Jobs and identity are so closely related that, for many people, losing a job is a little like losing a part of themselves. They feel that they have been left behind and that they have no way of showing their worth. Their lives seem to have no purpose any more.

When it comes to getting a job, depression can become a self-fulfilling prophecy. You don't get a job because you don't make enough effort to complete the application form properly, or you don't prepare yourself for the interview thoroughly enough. Having failed to land a job on a couple of occasions you begin to believe that you will never succeed. 'Why bother trying? They won't give me the job anyway.' When it gets to this stage, the odds are stacked against you.

Depression is easier to avoid than to cure. No matter how hard things become you must remember that work is only one aspect of your life and that there are other things which are important to you. Make every effort to get a job, but keep up your other interests as much as you can. Stay in contact with friends and family and make a point of looking for new activities. Try also to put something pleasant into each day. Listening to a particular radio programme; tackling a prize crossword; having a treat to eat – it needn't be a costly one. Don't discount voluntary work either. If you are between jobs, your skills, even on a temporary basis, would be greatly appreciated by a wide range of charitable, educational or sporting groups. You won't be paid, but you'll earn respect and you'll keep your interest in the outside world. It could give you something to talk about at interviews too!

Difficult questions

If you are facing an **interview** and are having trouble sleeping at night the chances are that two questions will be keeping you awake:

1. 'What sort of things will they ask me?'
2. 'Will I make a complete idiot of myself?'

You can rest assured that you won't have been invited to an interview just so that the interviewer can humiliate you. Employers are busy people and they have a wide range of applicants to choose from, so if you are invited to an interview, you can be fairly confident that you have at least some of the skills and qualities required.

On that basis, the majority of questions you are likely to be asked will be straightforward enough. A few may be tricky but there are several steps you can take to minimise risks.

First, study the job description and make sure that you know all the things that you will be responsible for. Then find examples in your experience to date which you can use to illustrate your ability to carry out the tasks that would be required of you.

Second, before the interview, find out as much as you can about the company. Is it a traditional set-up or is it run along more radical lines? What is important to the company – speed? accuracy? patience?

Third, use spare moments to think about the types of question you may be asked and the kinds of response you could make. Ask a friend to give you a 'mock' interview and tell you how you performed.

Finally, remember that an interview is a two-way process. Make a checklist of your strong points and take every opportunity to make sure that the interviewer is aware of them before you leave the room. Use the interview to your own advantage, making positive statements all along the way. If, for example, you are asked a technical question and you don't know the answer, be honest, but make a point of saying that you would be pleased to attend any training courses which the company could arrange for you.

Remember, you've done well to get this far and so there is no reason to fear the next part of the selection process. Whatever the outcome, you will leave the interview room with the same qualities and skills which you had when you entered half an hour earlier. If you are offered the job it will be because you have the most appropriate mix of skills and qualities for that company at that time. If you are turned down it won't mean that you are a failure. No matter whether you get the job or not, you come out of the interview no worse than when you went in. See also **Open and closed questions**.

Further information
Great Answers to Tough Interview Questions, 3rd edition, Martin John Yate (Kogan Page, 1992)

Disability

One of the most common reasons given by employers for not employing disabled people is that they have no suitable jobs. A recent survey of employers in Sussex found that 41 per cent thought that their field of work was unsuitable for disabled people. Other employers in the same occupational areas, however, thought that disabled people would be suitable. Clearly, there are some myths and prejudices which need to be confronted. The worst myths about disabled people suggest that they are less productive and have poor sickness records. This is not true. Having studied the work records of 48,000 disabled people, US researchers in 1948 came to the conclusion that there was no difference in productivity, absenteeism or safety records between disabled and able-bodied workers.

Enlightened employers willing to give disabled people a chance seem to be pleased with the results. A survey in Devon showed that 93 per cent of employers who had disabled people in their workforce thought that they performed as well as or better than able-bodied workers;

43 per cent reported that their attitude to work was better and 70 per cent felt that disabled workers' attendance was good. Twenty-six per cent thought it was better.

If you are disabled this should be enough to convince you that there is nothing wrong with disabled workers in general – or you in particular. Disability may make it difficult for you to carry out some tasks but there will probably be a wide range of other jobs which you could tackle without a second thought. The real problem lies with employers who seem unable to appreciate that there are few jobs suited only to people without any degree of disability.

When you are seeking employment, you can strengthen your case by emphasising all the things which you *can* do and then simply stating what, if any, special or extra facilities you need. If you have been in touch with a specialist careers adviser or if you are known to a particular **Jobcentre** interviewer, it can sometimes help to ask if they would be prepared to act as an intermediary on your behalf. In this way, you can suggest that an employer phones the interviewer if he needs further information about your abilities.

In law, the Disabled Persons (Employment) Acts of 1944 and 1958 require employers with more than 20 staff to employ a quota of registered disabled people. The current quota is 3 per cent. In 1992, however, only 20 per cent met their quota. Only ten prosecutions have ever been brought for failure to comply with the requirements of this law and no company has been prosecuted since 1975. The government argues that with only 1 per cent of the workforce registered as disabled, companies cannot possibly meet their quota, and therefore it would be unfair to prosecute. Why, therefore, do so many disabled people choose not to register their disability? There are probably a number of reasons. Undoubtedly, many feel that they have a better chance of gaining employment by not drawing attention to their disability.

As an individual looking for a job, only you can decide whether to register or not. Either way, whatever strategy you choose to adopt, you will need to take a positive attitude and show beyond any doubt that you are capable of carrying out all the employer's requirements. You may find it useful to quote some of the statistics mentioned above. You could also offer to demonstrate your abilities to any doubting employer.

Young disabled people can often obtain advice and help from specialist careers officers working for the local education authority.

Further information

There is a specialist employment agency for disabled people. The central office is in London but there is also a network of regional offices around the country. Lists of addresses and telephone numbers can be obtained from: Opportunities for People with Disabilities, 74 Great Portland Street, London W1N 5AL; 0171-726 4961

The Royal Association for Disability and Rehabilitation (RADAR) has several factsheets and brochures offering information and advice for disabled people. Publications include:

Working From Home, a guide for disabled people wishing to work at home. *Into Work*, information and advice on all matters concerned with seeking employment. RADAR can be contacted at: 12 City Forum, 250 City Road, London EC1V 8AF; 0171-250 3222

Distance learning

If you find that the training course you want is not available locally, it might be worth considering a distance learning package. The Open University is perhaps the most well-known form of distance learning. It offers a range of courses up to first degree level and beyond to people who study mainly at home. They learn through completing assignments and modules of study based on TV programmes and written material which is posted to them. Many courses have a two-week residential summer school component so that students can meet each other, learn together briefly and reduce the sense of isolation which can result from study at home.

Many distance learning schemes are highly sophisticated and there is an increasing range of supported self-study packages. Some use interactive video and computer programs as teaching methods. Telephone and fax messages enable students to enjoy almost instantaneous dialogue with tutors and these technological advances have eradicated many of the problems of time and distance associated with more traditional correspondence courses.

Distance learning offers you the chance to gain skills and qualifications from home. You can work at your own pace and start a course whenever you want. Some are expensive but if you are confident that you can gain the qualification and that it will help you to get a job, it might be worth taking out a **career development loan**.

The National Extension College (NEC) is one of the more successful distance learning colleges in the UK. Currently it offers 22 GCSE and 21 A level courses. In addition, it is also possible to study a range of courses in management, accountancy and office skills, counselling and voluntary work, or languages. Through the NEC you can even gain a University of London degree.

Distance learning, however, has its drawbacks. There is no regular class to attend so there may be less pressure to complete assignments by a particular time. Despite the best efforts of many distance learning tutors, it can be difficult to make and maintain relationships with fellow students. Without their support, distance learning can be a lonely road to follow. If you want to succeed you have to be highly motivated with a high level of self-discipline.

Further information
The Association of British Correspondence Colleges, 6 Francis Grove, London SW19 4DT; 0181-544 9559

The Council for the Accreditation of Correspondence Colleges, 27 Marylebone Road, London NW1 5JS; 0171-935 5391

The National Extension College, 18 Brooklands Avenue, Cambridge CB2 2HN; 01223-316644

The Open University, Walton Hall, Milton Keynes MK7 6AG; 01908 653231

The Open Learning Directory (available at major public libraries or at your Jobcentre.

Dress

There is an appropriate form of dress for every job and an appropriate form of dress for every job **interview** but they aren't necessarily the same. In general, you should dress more formally for an interview than for your day-to-day work. Teachers, for example, would normally wear a suit for interview, although many of them wouldn't wear one in the classroom. An office worker would be expected to wear a suit at interview but other types of worker might dress a little less formally. Most employers, however, expect to see male interviewees wearing trousers, jacket, shirt and tie. Jeans and tee shirts are not appropriate. Even if you're looking for a job on a building site, you must show an employer that you have made an effort to dress appropriately. It's a sign of respect for the interviewer, and a signal that you are serious in your wish to get the job. Some employers take the view that scruffy clothes are an indication of the type of work they can expect from the wearer. So, whatever job you go for, it is essential that your clothes are clean and neatly pressed. Women should avoid wearing too much jewellery or make-up.

Whenever possible, try to wear 'day-time' clothes without strong patterns. High fashion styles of dress can be difficult to wear and they can distract an interviewer. Your shoes should be comfortable and well polished.

An interviewee for a technician's post recently wore socks with 'happy birthday' printed on them. A quick check of his application form indicated that he had celebrated his birthday three days ago. He didn't get the job!

Further information
The Image Factor: A Guide to Effective Self-Presentation for Career Enhancement, Eleri Sampson (Kogan Page, 1994)

Employment history

Keep a record of your jobs. You'll need the information because most **application forms** ask you to list, with dates, all the organisations you have worked for. You'll also need the information to put on your **curriculum vitae**.

It is also a good idea to keep separate notes about particular tasks, events or special responsibilities that you have had during your working life. At one time, perhaps, you may have had to lead a team of people on a special project. At another time, you may have had to take on extra responsibilities when your boss was absent through illness or during a period of company reorganisation. Perhaps there have been times when you needed to take hard decisions or deal with particularly difficult situations. Note down too those times when you feel you achieved particular success. You wouldn't want to write all this down to send to an employer, of course, but many interviewers like to ask about previous experience so, by reading through your notes before the interview, you will be able to draw on examples which you can use to explain that you have the necessary background and experience for this job.

Be prepared also to explain why you left particular organisations. There may be one or two jobs which you didn't like, but interviewers prefer to hear positive statements so try to think of a couple of good points about each job.

Take a good look at your employment history and try to predict concerns and questions which it might prompt from an interviewer.

- Have you had lots of jobs for relatively short periods?
- Was there a positive reason for this?
- Has your work been largely within the same field, or have you had lots of different jobs?
- Is there a common theme to the work you have done?
- Is your experience limited to working within one organisation or have you simply never settled anywhere for long?
- Are there any gaps in your employment history?

Perhaps you took time out to raise a family or travel, or were self-employed for a while, or experienced a period of unemployment. With a little thought you can emphasise the positive aspects of all your previous history and use your past experience to show why your application for this job is a strong one. If you are just leaving school or college, mention work experience, or any Saturday or holiday work you have undertaken, and don't forget to let an employer know about any voluntary work you have done.

Equal opportunities

This is a term which implies that all people should be treated equally and fairly. When it comes to getting a job an equal opportunity employer will make efforts to ensure that he appoints the best person he can find irrespective of ethnic background, religious belief, gender or disability. Many employers go to great lengths to try to ensure that their appointment procedures are fair to all applicants so their **application forms** frequently ask for details of candidates' backgrounds. By keeping a careful check on the applications received and the people they appoint, employers are able to ensure that no particular type of person is favoured over another.

Often, organisations use **person specifications** to ensure that no candidate is excluded from consideration for a job without a sound and logical reason. Person specifications list the background, experience, skills and qualifications required of the successful candidate. People who meet these requirements should be considered for the job irrespective of who they are. Increasingly, age is being seen as an equal opportunity issue too.

People support equal opportunities in employment because they believe that it is right to do so. Why should anyone make assumptions about you simply on the strength of a little knowledge about gender, age or skin colour? There is also a sound economic argument for supporting equal opportunities in the workplace. An employer needs the best staff he can possibly attract. He doesn't do himself any favours by ignoring applications on the grounds of irrational prejudice. An employer who decides that he will not consider a woman for a post in his organisation has effectively chosen to ignore half of the potential candidates. With few exceptions, where gender may be a genuine occupational qualification (GOQ), he cannot possibly be sure that the most appropriate person for the job will be found in the remaining half of the population which he is prepared to consider.

Equal opportunities is an umbrella term for a number of Acts of Parliament. There is no single equal opportunity law and there is nothing in the law which states that any organisation has to be an equal opportunity employer. All companies, however, must as a minimum fulfil the requirements of a number of laws which make employment discrimination against certain groups illegal.

The Equal Pay Act 1970 (amended in 1983) stipulates that an employee is entitled to equal pay (and other contractual terms and conditions) with an employee of the opposite sex if they are doing work which is the same or broadly similar, or if the work they do has been rated as equivalent by job evaluation or in terms of the demands made on the worker.

The Sex Discrimination Acts of 1975 and 1986 make it unlawful to discriminate:

- in the arrangements made for deciding who is offered a job;
- in the terms on which the job is offered;
- in deciding who is offered the job;
- in making opportunities available for promotion, transfer or training;
- in the benefits, facilities or services granted to employees;
- in dismissals or other unfavourable treatment of employees.

The Race Relations Act 1976 makes it unlawful to discriminate against anyone because of race, colour, nationality, ethnic or national origins. The Act applies to jobs and training as well as housing and education.

Further information

The Equal Opportunities Commission is concerned mainly with ensuring equality of opportunity in employment, education and training for men and women. The address is: Overseas House, Quay Street, Manchester M3 3HN; 0161-833 9244

The Commission for Racial Equality has offices in London, Leicester, Birmingham, Manchester, Leeds and Edinburgh. The headquarters address is: Elliot House, 10–12 Allington Street, London SW1E 5EH; 0171-828 7022

The Royal Association for Disability and Rehabilitation's address is: 12 City Forum, 250 City Road, London EC1V 8AF; 0171-250 3222

Essential equipment

In some jobs, you will be expected to provide your own equipment. Nurses, for example, are often required to buy their own lapel watches, chefs have their own knives and many tradespeople have their own collection of tools. One employer asks whether prospective woodworking employees have their own equipment. He isn't being miserly; he feels that anyone committed to their craft would have their own collection of tools and take pride in them.

When you are jobhunting there is also a list of essential equipment which you must have if you are to be effective. Getting a job is a serious business which involves hard work and effort. It is a job in itself and, like any task, it can be made easier if you have the right tools and equipment to hand.

As a minimum you need a notebook and pencil with you at all times. You may hear of a job through a chance conversation in the supermarket or in the bus queue. A notebook and pencil mean that you don't need to rely on your memory. You can note down names, addresses, telephone numbers and directions immediately.

Checklists are also essential items of equipment. They enable you to plan your day or week to make sure that you are doing everything at the right time and on schedule for any appointments or interviews.

Local newspapers provide essential information about job vacancies so you need to see every issue on the day it is published. Either buy one or visit the local library and read it there. There are probably also one or two magazines which publish advertisements for the type of job you want so these will be essential reading too. Telephone directories and Yellow Pages will enable you to discover employers' names, addresses and telephone numbers so keep copies in the house.

At home you need a supply of envelopes and writing paper. Keep your stationery simple and plain. Use A4 paper and simple business envelopes. Photocopy paper is cheaper and heavier than typing paper. Small sheets of coloured notepaper, with designs and motifs on them, are fine for writing to friends but don't use them when you are trying to get a job. This is a serious business and you need to use business-style stationery. Make sure too that you have a supply of stamps and access to a telephone. A phone card and some coins in your pocket mean that you can chase up opportunities without effort and, thanks to the notebook and pencil in your pocket, you can scribble down appointments as you speak to potential employers.

A good **curriculum vitae**, a **letter of application**, and an enquiry letter which you can copy and adapt to suit individual jobs are also essential tools for the business of getting a job. Spend time getting them right and checking spellings, as you can expect to use them again and again. If you can put them on a word processor, they can be printed in large quantities without much effort. Alternatively, you may have to copy them out each time, in which case a good pen also becomes an essential item of equipment.

Finally, you need to have an **address** where you can be contacted easily. If you are living in a hostel or lodgings, or if your address is a student hall of residence which is only useful during term-time, you may need to rely on family or close friends to keep mail and take messages for you. Whatever arrangements you make, the responsibility for maintaining close contact will be yours. Don't blame family or friends if you miss a job opportunity because you failed to contact them for a couple of weeks.

Experience

Experience can count for a great deal. You can use it to support your job application by illustrating how you have succeeded in similar situations in the past. If necessary, you can argue that your past experience compensates for your lack of formal qualifications. Careful recording of past experience can even be used to support your bid for gaining qualifications through the **accreditation of prior learning**.

But experience has its limitations. Experience in driving a steam train, for example, wouldn't count for much with British Rail today. Technical experience can quickly become out of date. Only two years after closing the shipyards in Sunderland, the government reported that there was a lack of skilled engineers in the region. Technology was advancing at such a rate that even this short time was enough to make the experience of local unemployed engineers out of date.

Similarly, managers in local government and the civil service, who worked throughout the 1970s, gained experience of working within growing organisations. They encountered massive problems in the 1980s, though, when they had to manage the reduction of services. Their experience of running organisations in the fat years was of little use when they were expected to make cuts.

To be of any value experience needs to have been positive. On some people, it has a negative effect. Through experience, they may know how to spin a job out or how to take short cuts. They may have learned how to get by with the minimum of effort or energy. In effect, experience can produce cynical individuals, resistant to development and unwilling to make any effort beyond the minimum required.

You need to show an employer that your experience is positive and relevant. You can do this by looking back through your employment history and picking out incidents, jobs and tasks which challenged you and enabled you to learn lessons which are important to the job you are applying for.

It is also worth remembering that, while technical skill has a short 'sell by date', experience of handling people has a longer-term value. Whatever you do, the chances are that the way you relate to people will be an important aspect of the job. As a working member of an organisation your experience of people will be worthwhile and you shouldn't overlook this. Remember, too, that your experience in this area need not have come directly from work. Even if you have only a short employment history, you may be able to find examples from other parts of your life which can illustrate your skill with people.

First impressions

First impressions are often made at a subconscious level. They are based on a range of clues about an individual which are collected and sifted within minutes of first encountering them. Instantaneously almost, the brain analyses information about dress, speech, posture and facial expression to make an instant judgement.

Some people say that first impressions can be remarkably accurate and they put a great deal of faith in them. Others argue that it is better to keep an open mind before forming an opinion. Either way, when you are trying to get a job, it can only do you good to make a favourable first impression. When going for an interview, be pleasant and polite to everyone you meet; apart from anything else it gives the impression that you'd be nice to work with. Don't just save this pleasantness for the interview room, however; remember, receptionists and secretaries may have been asked to let the interviewers know what they thought of you on arrival.

Most employers will have a picture in their minds of an ideal candidate. At interview, they'll be looking for the person who appears to match the picture most closely. When you are trying to get a job, your task is to gain enough background knowledge of the organisation and the job, so that you can act the part. If you are polite and enthusiastic and if you look and sound like a person who does this kind of work, you'll create a good first impression. See also **Dress**.

Fit for work

You don't have to be a perfect physical specimen to get a job, but you have to be fit enough to carry out the tasks involved. Work forces a kind of discipline on you but when you are out of work and looking for a job it's easy to let things slide. You can stay up watching the late-night movie because you don't have to be up early in the morning. You can spend an hour lying on the settee reading the paper because it kills time, and you can pop into the pub for lunch because you don't want to be bothered with cooking for yourself. Being unemployed can also set you apart from friends who are still in work so your sporting and social interests decline.

Medical surveys have confirmed that unemployment can have harmful effects on health. Your level of fitness can deteriorate quickly but, more important perhaps, long before any serious long-term damage is done, you begin to look unfit. First impressions are important so if you want to succeed at interview, use your time constructively. Develop a daily routine, keep up your sporting and social interests, investigate training possibilities, undertake some voluntary work, and make sure that you remain fit for work. See also **Depression**, **Health**.

Four minutes

Many interviews last about half an hour and many interviewers are fairly inexperienced. If you have had three interviews recently, you may have more experience of the process than a large number of employers who take on no more than one or two staff each year. Research suggests that, without realising it, inexperienced or untrained interviewers spend about four minutes trying to get to know you. Within that time they form an opinion about you and your suitability for the job. Then, for the remaining 26 minutes, they inadvertently ask questions which seek to confirm or deny their initial feelings.

Freelancing

This is a form of self-employment where you sell your skills to others, undertaking short-term contracts for whichever organisation happens to need you at a given time. Because you are self-employed, you represent no drain on their resources during quiet times. Many companies rely heavily on freelances. It is a way of reducing in-house staff while enabling them to call on the expertise of a wide range of specialists.

Like all forms of self-employment, the freelance life can be precarious. Sometimes you may have more demands for your services than you can cope with; at other times, you may have no work at all. Despite this, freelancing has certain attractions. As a self-employed person, you have some control over which jobs to tackle and which to leave alone. You can also undertake as much or as little work as you wish and you can schedule your work to suit other priorities in your life. Many freelances are able to work from home and, for them, this was a significant factor in their career decision. If your ultimate goal is permanent full-time work within a company, a period of freelance

> Dear Sir,
>
> I am a freelance alarm installer. I guarantee the highest standards of work (British Standard and NACOSS) in the installation of fire, security alarms and door entry systems.
>
> I am able to work on a day-work basis of £10.00 per hour, or quotations for individual jobs can be negotiated.
>
> No business can afford to 'carry' surplus staff these days, so in an ideal world you should be free to increase or decrease your level of staffing to meet changes in demand for your services. In effect, workers should be available when you want them. During quieter periods, you should be free to reduce your staff levels to reflect reduced demand. I am able to meet your requirements. Call on me when you are busy and, during quieter periods, let me go!
>
> Payment on satisfactory completion of work brings you the benefit of satisfied customers and an organisational structure flexible enough to enable you to increase your customer base without enlarging your permanent staffing commitment.
>
> Please keep my name, address and telephone number on file. Should you wish to discuss my proposal further, don't hesitate to contact me at the above address.

work will enable you to become known and show your worth to a number of companies wishing to expand their permanent workforce or replace a retiring member of staff some time in the future. When it comes to getting a full-time job, the quality of your work as a freelance is probably the best reference you can obtain.

Last year, a redundant security alarm installer wrote a letter similar to the one above. He sent it to a number of companies listed in Yellow Pages.

On the strength of the letter and subsequent discussions with company managers, he has negotiated contracts which have kept him employed throughout the year. He has been offered full-time permanent employment on three occasions and has turned down every offer. Having tasted the freedom of self-employment, he is reluctant to give up his freelance status.

Further information
Going Freelance: A Guide to Self-Employment with Minimum Capital, 4th edition, Godfrey Golzen (Kogan Page, 1993)

Further education

Traditionally, colleges of further education provided work-related courses while local adult education institutions concentrated on non-vocational learning. These days the traditional divide between learning for work and learning for pleasure is becoming increasingly blurred. A welding course may be useful to someone hoping to get a job in a car bodywork repair shop, but it could be equally interesting to someone hoping to build a boat in their spare time. Languages can be used for business or pleasure, and someone wanting to learn word processing may need the skill for their job or because they are the secretary of a voluntary group.

College courses can be the key to developing the skills you need to gain employment. They are available for people of any age, and the rate of change is such that it is becoming increasingly accepted that training and retraining are a normal aspect of daily life. Such courses can bridge the gap between the skills you have now and the skills you need to get the job you seek. College staff should also be able to advise you about higher education possibilities and gaining recognition for the skills and experience you have already acquired.

Many courses are organised on a day-release basis and students are released from their jobs or training placements to attend. There are a confusing number of examining bodies and qualifications available at present but, as more industries develop NVQs, the picture should become simpler. Young people can get information and advice about educational opportunities beyond the age of 16 from careers officers, careers teachers in schools and by contacting colleges directly.

Whatever subject you are thinking of studying, it is worth checking out what's on offer in local colleges. Addresses, telephone numbers and further details of nearby colleges will be available at your local public library.

G

General Certificate of Education

GCEs. These are otherwise known as O (ordinary) levels and **A** (advanced) **levels**. O level examinations were usually taken at 16 years of age. They tested knowledge of a fairly traditional range of school subjects and were seen as the gateway to further education or 'good' jobs. Five 'O' level passes including maths and English were the goal to which many school pupils and their parents aspired. The last O level examinations in UK schools took place in 1987. They have been superseded by GCSEs (**General Certificates of Secondary Education**). At one time, they were the 'gold standard' against which other examinations were judged. Few other public examinations have been held in such high esteem by employers so, if you've got a few O levels, put them on your application form and let people know.

General Certificate of Secondary Education

GCSEs are the current standard by which many young people are judged at the end of their compulsory school life. They replaced earlier GCE and CSE certificates which came under increasing criticism from many educationalists, who argued that CSEs were undervalued because of the continued existence of the older more traditional GCE O levels.

Many employers still place great value on the old GCE examination. They view GCSE grade C as an O level equivalent, and as a result they tend to pay particular attention to subjects where a young person has scored grade C and above. Four or five grade C GCSEs can be the key to a wide range of job or further education opportunities, provided Maths and English are among them. On the other hand, few jobs require you to be good at English Literature *and* Biology *and* Media Studies *and* Computer Studies *and* Art and Design. In a letter of application or a CV you can emphasise your strengths by writing 'my best subjects were Media Studies and Art and Design

(GCSE Grade B). I also took Computer Studies and English Literature (Grade D) and Biology (Grade E).'

From a young jobseeker's point of view, GCSEs can be a double-edged sword. Under the older GCE system you passed or failed: either you got an O level or you didn't. Failure was no disgrace because the system was designed to ensure that the majority of people didn't get them. With GCSEs there is a broad band of grades that tell an employer how good or how bad you are.

For adults wishing to pick up qualifications, GCSEs are probably inappropriate. There is a variety of work-related qualifications which will probably carry more credibility with an employer. If you are intent on gaining traditional qualifications, though, GCSEs are available through evening classes and colleges of further education.

General National Vocational Qualification

GNVQs are new qualifications which offer an alternative route to higher education or employment. Each GNVQ is designed to test skills and knowledge within a broad area of work. With GCSE and A levels you tend to study fairly standard school subjects. A GNVQ, however, offers you the possibility of gaining a qualification in something more closely related to the world of work. The earliest GNVQs were offered in the fields of art and design, business, health and social care, leisure and tourism, and manufacturing. Further subject areas are being added all the time. Currently, there are two levels of GNVQ on offer. Later it is hoped that five levels will be developed. Levels 1, 2 and 3 will be known as 'Foundation', 'Intermediate' and 'Advanced' GNVQ. Level 4 will be roughly equivalent to the level of study required of someone in their first year of university and level 5 will be pitched at postgraduate level.

Level 2 (Intermediate) is considered to be about the same standard as four good GCSEs and it normally takes a year to complete. Level 3 (Advanced) has been designed to be the equivalent of at least two A levels, but this is where the similarities end. GNVQs are radically different from most A levels.

GNVQs are made up of 'units', and each unit comprises a number of 'elements'. You attain a GNVQ by showing an assessor that you have attained the necessary skills or knowledge to meet the requirements of each element. At GNVQ level 2, for example, you would have to demonstrate your ability to use information technology. You attain this unit by showing that you can set up storage systems and input information, edit, organise and integrate information from different sources, select and use formats for presenting information, evaluate features and facilities of given applications, and deal with errors and faults on computers.

Each of the above is an element towards the information technology unit. With GNVQ your job is to collect evidence through project work, demonstration and study to show an assessor that you have gained the necessary skill and knowledge.

GNVQ students are able to work at their own pace and their own level. They are assessed on each element when they think they are ready. There is no formal end of course examination. Each student keeps a record and can be credited with having achieved each unit. Some may not complete the full range of units necessary for the award of a GNVQ, but their achievements will be recognised and they will be able to continue adding units to their portfolio of achievement through further education, should they wish to.

It has been argued that GNVQs combine the best features of A levels and NVQs. A person with a GNVQ will have the qualifications to continue studying and the skills to start work. As a new qualification, GNVQs have yet to be tested in the market-place. It is too early to gauge how employers will react to them. It is certain, however, that a great deal of government time and effort will be invested in promoting them. Already 90 per cent of higher education institutions will accept GNVQ level 3 as an alternative to A levels.

Grant-making trusts

If lack of training or qualifications stands between you and the job you wish to do, you could try to get a study grant or **career development loan**. The first port of call should be your local education authority. Staff there will be able to advise you on whether you qualify for a grant and the size and type of grant available for the course you wish to follow.

If you don't qualify for a grant from the local authority, don't despair. Go to the library reference section and get hold of the *Directory of Grant-making Trusts*. This book contains details of hundreds of organisations which make grants for a wide variety of reasons. Many will offer financial support to individuals for educational purposes.

The *Directory* is updated regularly and is a mine of useful information. It gives details of the areas of interest, the size of grant available, and any special restrictions or rules about its use. It also reveals how to apply for grants and when applications should be made. Some trusts help people living in a particular area. Some are available to support students with an interest in a particular field of study, but others are much less clearly defined and trustees are willing to consider applications from people with a wide range of interests.

You don't need to be poor to apply for many of these grants but you do need to be able to show how the grant would benefit you, the community or your chosen field of interest. Some grants are available to support study, but others can be used to support travel – to gain experience elsewhere, for example.

Further information
The Directory of Grant-making Trusts is published by the Charities Aid Foundation, 48 Pembury Road, Tonbridge, Kent TN9 2JD; 01732 771333

Grants

If your route to getting a job involves full-time higher education in order to gain a required qualification, you may be eligable for a student grant from your local education authority (LEA). There are two kinds of grant – mandatory and discretionary.

You are entitled to a mandatory grant if: (a) you attend an eligible course; and (b) you are personally eligible to receive one.

In general, a mandatory grant is available for any full-time advanced course provided it takes place at a UK university, a publicly funded college, or a specified private or NHS institution. Such courses must lead to a first degree such as a BA, a BSc or a BEd, a diploma of higher education, a postgraduate certificate of education, or a specified equivalent qualification.

To be eligible you must be an ordinary resident of the British Isles, and you must not have previously been on a higher education course for which you received help from public funds. There are, however, exceptions to this. Mandatory grants are available, for example, to people wishing to train as teachers following the successful completion of a first degree course.

Where mandatory grants are not available, LEAs may award discretionary grants. Each LEA sets its own rules in this matter and therefore you need local advice to gain further information.

Your LEA decides how much grant to give you by working out the maximum amount you are entitled to and then deciding how much contribution should be made by you, your parents, or your husband or wife. The size of the contribution is determined by their income. It is governed by national scales. The grant you receive from an LEA, therefore, is the maximum amount – minus any contributions.

If you are over 25, have been married for at least two years, or have been self-supporting for at least three years before the start of the academic year for which you are applying for a grant, you may be considered as an 'independent' student, in which case your parents' income will not be taken into account in determining the level of support.

GRANTS

Financial support for studies and high level research leading to Master's degrees and PhDs comes from a variety of sources. Higher-level degrees ceased to be included in LEA mandatory grants lists in 1989, and since then each LEA has done the best it can, with dwindling resourses, to continue to support students undertaking high-level study. Hampshire, for example, until recently was able to support students by contributing £1000 a year towards teaching costs.

The Department for Education funds studies in subjects such as art, design, journalism and museum studies. The British Academy funds study and research into a wide range of subjects including archaeology, architecture, languages and politics. A further six research councils act as funding bodies for study in particular areas of interest. Your LEA should be able to offer you advice on the most appropriate funding body for you. Alternatively, you could contact the Department for Education direct.

Further information

The Department for Education, Publications Centre, PO Box 2193, London E15 2EU; 0171-925 5000

The Scottish Office, Education Department, New St Andrews House, St James Centre, Edinburgh EH1 3SY; 0131-556 8400

Department of Education for Northern Ireland, Rathgael House, Balloo Road, Bangor, Co Down BT19 2PR; 01247-270077.

The Welsh Office, Training, Enterprise and Education Department, 4th Floor, Companies House, Crown Way, Cardiff CF4 3UT; 01222-380753

Locally, careers officers, careers teachers, staff in colleges or your local public library should be able to give you the address and telephone number of your LEA awards office. You can also consult the telephone directory.

Handwriting

Poor handwriting can cost you a job but you may never know it. If your name or address is hard to read, the further details and application forms you asked to be sent to you could go to the wrong address. Even worse, if your handwriting is really bad, the company could decide that responding to your letter isn't worth the price of a stamp. If you can't be bothered to write neatly and legibly, why should they bother trying to decipher your scrawl?

Neat handwriting is a skill which can be learned. It gets better with practice and it is considerably easier to write neatly if you know exactly what you are going to write. That way you can concentrate on forming the letters correctly rather than worrying about what the next word is going to be. So, if you are completing a form, take a photocopy and then read the instructions thoroughly. Does it tell you to use capital letters throughout? Begin by completing the photocopy of the form; if you make a mistake on the photocopy it won't matter. Keep your letters roughly the same size and make sure that your statements will fit in the space provided. If you are unsure of any spellings, use a dictionary and then get someone to read the form for you. When you are sure that it is exactly as you want it, copy it out again on the original application form. If you have to send the form off quickly or if you don't have access to a photocopier, complete the form in pencil so that you can rub out any mistakes before you go over it in black ink.

If your handwriting is really appalling it might be worth asking someone to type the letter or the form for you. At least that way you know that your words will be read and understood. Some employers, however, insist that applicants for jobs complete the forms and write the letters in their own handwriting. They believe that you can learn a lot about someone by the way they write. At such times, you have no choice. If you want the job, you'll do everything possible to make sure your application is neat. Think about the wages you could earn if you get this job. Isn't it worth making an effort?

Health

Some jobs require a certain level of fitness and physical strength. The majority, however, require no more than a reasonable degree of good health.

Different companies have different attitudes towards checking the health of their prospective employees. Some insist that all new employees are given a health check before they start work. Some even make the offer of employment subject to a satisfactory health check. In these cases it is best not to resign from your present job until you know that you have successfully passed the test.

But the cost of a full medical examination for every prospective new employee can be expensive, so some companies have developed alternative arrangements. Several local authorities, for example, have calculated that it is better to run health checks only on new recruits over 40 years old. Health problems in under 40-year-olds are relatively rare and so, statistically at least, they have found it cheaper to support members of staff under 40 who fall ill than it is to run a health check on every prospective employee in this age group.

Some companies don't submit anyone to a physical examination. Rather, they ask candidates to complete confidential health questionnaires which are sent to a medical officer who looks at the requirements of the job and assesses the risks. The questionnaire will ask about your height, weight and previous health history. In most instances the medical officer won't be bothered about recruiting super-fit staff. He may look closely at your weight, though, because obese employees are a bad risk for the pension scheme. In most cases he will simply be seeking to ensure that you are in a reasonable state of health and able to carry out the duties required of you.

If you have had a long period of illness and are worried that this may count against you in a job application, it may be worth speaking to your doctor or consultant to see if he would be prepared to give a confidential health reference to prospective employers. A note to this effect enclosed with your application may help to alleviate any fears which an employer may have.

Higher education

Where does higher education begin and how can it help you to get a job? Higher education is a term usually reserved for courses leading to HND or degree-level qualifications. Most people are 18 before they can embark on such courses. Many jobs require that you have undertaken higher education courses. Teachers, lawyers and veterinary surgeons, for example, are all required to have studied to degree level at least.

Some occupations require you to study particular courses related to the type of work you intend to take up. Other professions are happy to recruit staff educated to 'degree' level regardless of the subject studied. In these cases, the capability of high-level study is considered to be more important than the subject chosen. Someone wishing to be a primary school teacher, for example, could choose to study for a BEd. In effect, he would be studying 'education' at degree level and on completion of the course he would be a qualified teacher. Alternatively, he could study for any degree he chose, and then gain his teaching qualification by undertaking a one-year postgraduate course.

Higher education often involves full-time study away from home. There are study grants available for many courses, and if your chosen career requires a higher educational qualification, you will probably need to talk to a careers officer, or the grants office of your local education authority to see about the possibilities.

Although most students are over 18, there is no top limit on the age at which you can start to study for higher educational qualifications, and if the thought of leaving home to take up the student life for three years is more than you can bear, there is a wide range of other study options open to you. Many people gain their first degree through home-study as students of the Open University, others take advantage of distance learning opportunities and other flexible learning packages which are now widely available.

Most higher education institutions expect you to have attained an appropriate educational level before you begin to study for higher education qualifications. These minimum entry requirements are established to ensure that your background knowledge and ability are sufficiently developed for you to cope with the requirements of the course. A college or university will often make young people an offer of a place on a course dependent upon the achievement of certain grades at A level. Older people, however, can often be accepted for work-related courses on the strength of their background knowledge and experience gained in the workplace.

If the prospect of high-level study seems frightening, many local colleges and evening class centres run 'return to study' and 'access' courses. They can help you to develop your study skills and enable you to explore the higher educational opportunities which may be available to you.

Further information
How to Win as a Mature Student Teresa Rickards (Kogan Page,

1992), is a particularly useful book for anyone who has been out of full-time education for more than a couple of years.

Hobbies and interests

'Find something that you like to do and then get someone to pay you for doing it!' Many people manage to turn their particular interests into paid work. Sometimes they wouldn't have thought about the possibility of earning money through their hobby until they were faced with the prospect of unemployment. There are countless examples – the redundant coal miner who now paints portraits of pets in oils, the model train collector who makes a reasonable living out of buying and selling to other collectors, or the keep-fit fanatic who set up a dance and aerobics studio. For such people redundancy can be a liberating experience, a chance to get out of the rut, to reassess their values and start working for themselves rather than for the company or the factory. They wouldn't consider returning to their former employment.

Some people are even fortunate enough to find employers willing to pay them for work directly associated with their hobby. Model-makers are often in great demand. The armed forces, architects and engineers, museums and government departments – all require the skills of people who can translate plans, maps and photographs of terrain into three-dimensional scale models. The youth service is continually on the look-out for people who can enthuse about their area of interest and pass on their skills to others. Sportsmen and women find satisfying work as teachers, lecturers and leisure centre assistants, while DIY experts can easily convince a wide range of employers of their value.

Hobbies and interests can also help you to get a job not directly related to your activities out of work. They give an employer a useful insight into the kind of person you are. Hobbies and interests can indicate an ability to manage time effectively and draw a reasonable balance between the demands of the job and the need for a life beyond the office or factory gate.

At a deeper level, all jobs require a wide range of skills. Technical expertise is only part of the equation. An ability to relate to other people and to operate as a member of a team, the willingness to take on tasks and see them through – all these qualities are important in and out of work. Your interests outside work offer an important insight into the type of person you are.

Model-makers, for example, if they are any good, have an eye for detail and a degree of patience. Successful sportsmen and women must have drive, ambition, and an inner strength which sustains them and keeps them aiming for ever more difficult targets. Coaches and local team managers have to be interested in people in order to build teams and motivate their players. Charity workers, members of clubs and voluntary organisations often have a strong sense of loyalty and commitment to their community. An employer will often look at a person's hobbies and interests to see if the qualities suggested by such interests match the qualities he is looking for in his ideal candidate. If there appears to be a match, he may look for ways in which they could be harnessed and channelled to suit the job requirements.

Be careful, however, when you list your hobbies and interests. If your list is too long, an employer may wonder how you can find time for work with so many outside interests. Be careful also to be accurate in the description of your interests. You are likely to be asked questions at interview. One woman came unstuck at an interview recently when she included 'military history' among her interests on the application form. She meant Second World War history and so was taken aback when the interviewer began chatting to her about Napoleon!

Identity

'Who you are' has a lot to do with 'what you do'. Take a look in any newspaper: 'Thirty-seven year old John Smith, a plumber from . . . ', 'Primary school teacher Mrs Julie Whittel said today . . . ', 'The heavens opened for airline pilot Chris Price yesterday when . . . '. A job offers a sense of identity.

At work or on holiday you look and act according to a set of unwritten yet fairly rigid rules based on what the media and the community expect of you. People react to a stereotype image of people in their jobs. An undertaker, for example, would be expected to look and behave differently from a primary school teacher. A university professor may not need to dress as neatly as an accountant. Jobs are about earning money but they are also about a number of other things. When you have a job, you have a place in society, a value and a sense of identity. When you are trying to get a job money is important but it isn't the only consideration. If you were a secretary, who would you prefer to work for – a scrap metal merchant or a film company? The conditions of work may be roughly the same and the pay may be better at the scrap metal merchant's, but many people would work for less if they could get a job with the film company. On a Friday evening they would prefer to tell their friends that they work for Warner Brothers rather than Acme Iron Recovery Ltd.

When you're thinking about applying for a job, ask yourself how you would feel about being a member of this profession or company. Teaching may be fun during the week and the paid holidays seem attractive but could you live up to society's expectations outside work? Does the type of work you seek 'fit' your particular type of personality or are you going to spend your working life feeling as if you are wearing a straitjacket?

When it comes to losing a job, the longer-term loss of identity can be more damaging than the immediate loss of income. As you walk out of the building for the last time you can feel as if you have lost more than a wage. Somehow you have been robbed of your identity and sense of worth. Out of work you are undervalued and de-skilled, and you feel as if you have no way of proving your worth to anyone. You have lost all the benefits of employment but, in trying to preserve your sense of identity, the straitjacket remains.

When you have been out of work even for a short time, the possibility of regaining employment can seem as remote as climbing Everest unaided – and it isn't only the unemployed who feel this way. Anyone who has been out of mainstream paid employment will begin to question their worth in the workplace, and these doubts arise at the worst possible moment – just when you are trying to convince an employer that you are worth investing in!

There is no easy or obvious solution to the problem but, if work is important to you, getting a job must be approached in a disciplined and businesslike way. You are no less a person when you are out of work, but if you want to be successful in your jobhunt you mustn't allow unemployment to hurt you. At such times you need to be more disciplined and energetic than ever before. Allocate time to finding work and exploring all the possibilities in a systematic and thorough way. Just as important, allocate some time to preserving and maintaining your identity. Keep up those hobbies and interests, maintain contacts with friends and former colleagues, undertake some voluntary work or training if it will help but, above all, stay busy and make sure that your activity is purposeful. Find a way of holding on to those things in your life which you can feel good about.

Income

Successful organisations are those which can change and adapt to new developments in the market-place and, in order to get the kind of flexibility needed, many managers now prefer to employ people on a short-term basis. Some also prefer their workforce to contain a high proportion of staff on part-time contracts. So you may need to consider making up your income from a variety of sources. Perhaps you need to consider getting two part-time jobs rather than one full-time. Perhaps you could consider a part-time job to supplement freelance work. Perhaps a short-term full-time contract could get you through a difficult period when income from your own business is low. Whatever the future holds the variety of work arrangements is sure to expand. In the same way that companies are adapting to changing circumstances, you may also need to take a flexible approach to creating your income.

Initiative

Not long ago one Friday afternoon there was a job advertised in a local paper for someone to work in a small travel agent's. The company needed someone to work in their office, preferably able to speak French.

One likely candidate, with a degree in French, spent an entire weekend preparing a letter of application and a CV. His application arrived at the travel agent's office on the Tuesday morning and the following day he received a note thanking him for his application but explaining that the job had already been filled!

While he had been busy preparing his letter, someone else had dashed home, thrown on a suit and tapped on the door of the travel agent's office with a standard CV tucked under his arm. He had some knowledge of French and was able to convince the travel agent that he would enjoy the prospect of improving his skill through evening classes in his own time. When the office closed that Friday afternoon the travel agent went home pleased that his advertisement had been so effective. He had a new enthusiastic member of staff starting on Monday morning!

Flair and energy added together make initiative. People who get jobs are not necessarily the best, but they are able to use their initiative to ensure that they are in the right place at the right time with the right equipment. They make their own luck. Direct contact with employers can give you a head start in the race to find work, but don't restrict yourself to contacting employers who are advertising for staff, take the initiative and speak to all employers who may one day need your skills. Many companies don't need to advertise for staff, they are able to recruit from a pool of people they know who have already expressed an interest in working for them. If that doesn't produce results, take the bull by the horns and put an ad in the paper. There may be an employer out there who doesn't realise how much he needs you!

In-service training

When you are trying to get a job, it is always helpful if you can show a prospective employer that your skills are up to date, that you have a track record of training, and that you enjoy learning more about your chosen field.

For that reason, whatever job you are in, make sure that your boss knows you would welcome the opportunity to develop your skills and widen your experience. Whatever training you do, keep a record and use it to update your CV.

Training isn't only about being sent on courses, however. You can also learn a great deal by looking over someone else's shoulder, or swapping aspects of your job with someone. There are great benefits to an organisation if many of its staff can become skilled in a number of areas. The benefits for you are obvious too, so it makes a great deal of sense if you think of your development in work as a kind of partnership between you and your employer. Your boss may not realise it but it is in both your interests to work together on this. You may have to give up some of your own time and, on occasion, you may have to spend some of your own money, but think of it as an investment in yourself – it moves you closer to that ideal job which you have always wanted.

Some employers may be prepared to offer financial assistance towards meeting the cost of outside courses which you would like to take. If, for any reason, an employer is unable to allow you time out of work to attend a course, it may be possible to study the same subject through a distance learning package or at another college where it is scheduled to take place outside work time.

Interest

Genuine interest in a job is attractive to employers. If you are interested your skill and productivity will increase as time goes on, you will enjoy training and you will probably be keen to keep up to date with the latest methods and techniques used in the job. Interested workers usually make good colleagues, they are happy in their work so there is less friction in the workplace. With an interested workforce an employer has to worry less about supervision, quality control and productivity.

At interview an employer will often ask candidates why they are interested in the job. It's an obvious question, and yet a surprising number of people have difficulty in answering it.

Think about all the various aspects of the job and list them.

- Does the job require you to work alone or as a member of a team?
- Does it require you to investigate problems and solve them?
- Does the work take place in an office or outside?
- Will you be expected to travel?
- Does it involve working with your hands?
- Will you be expected to handle complicated machinery?
- Does the job carry a great deal of responsibility?

Make your list in two columns: Likes and Dislikes, and hope that there will be more under 'likes' than 'dislikes'. You can use some of the 'likes' to explain why the job interests you.

If you find that your checklist contains more dislikes than likes, you should think again about pursuing this particular job. You might be better suited to some other kind of work. This is particularly important when you are just starting your career; your earnings may be low and you may be expected to put in a good deal of study. If you aren't interested in the job, you probably won't see the course out and you won't qualify.

As someone going into a job for the first time, you have to use your strong interest in the job to counterbalance the fact that you will be lacking in skill and experience. By showing a great deal of interest in the work, and by being able to explain where that interest comes from, you should be able to convince a potential employer that you will learn the required skills quickly and easily.

Interview technique *See* Interviews

Interview technique is about pulling together a range of skills and strategies to make sure that the efforts you have made so far are well received by the interviewer. **Jobclubs** and a number of consultants in the private sector can offer valuable training. In school and college 'mock' interviews are an excellent way of practising for the real event. Interview technique can also be learned through experience. Whether you get the job or not, you can use every interview to practise and hone your skills in this area.

When you have an interview, arrive early, having checked the route and transport beforehand. Let the receptionist know who you are and ask if there is somewhere you can leave your coat and bag. The less encumbered you are the better. You'll probably be asked to take a seat and wait. If you've done your preparation well, you'll be smartly and appropriately dressed, and you'll already know quite a bit about the job you are chasing and you'll have done lots of research about the company. You may feel nervous but you are well prepared and they haven't invited you here to waste your time or theirs.

In the few minutes before you enter the interview room, run through the questions you think you may be asked and rehearse your model answers for the last time. Try to relax by sitting comfortably and breathing in and out slowly. Read a magazine or chat to the receptionist. She may have been asked to let the interviewers know her impression of you, so make a good impression and use this time to gain as much new information about the company as you can. Is it a busy, chaotic sort of place or is there a sense of calm and purpose? How do people greet each other here? What seems to be the main topic of conversation? A degree of nervousness can help to ensure that you perform well so, if you feel a little jittery, remind yourself that this can work positively for you.

When you are invited into the interview room, smile pleasantly at your interviewers and shake hands. Wait until you are asked to sit down, and then sit comfortably with your hands on your lap; try not to fidget. The first question will probably be an 'icebreaker', something easy to settle you down and get the conversation moving. Speak clearly and steadily and act as naturally as you can. Don't try to change your accent or use unfamiliar words; you won't be able to keep the act up for long. The chances are that you have already prepared your answer to this question so you can concentrate on making a good first impression. If there are several interviewers, make sure that you look at each one as you speak. Make eye contact and engage their attention. By looking at your interviewers you will make them feel that you are talking to them, not repeating a rehearsed speech.

Interviews are false, unnatural events where strangers have only half an hour or so to decide whether they can work together for several years. Throughout the interview try to project a 'pleasant' version of yourself. You need to convince the employer that you can do the job, but you mustn't appear boastful. Being pleasant, however, doesn't mean that you should agree with everything he says. The interviewer wants to appoint someone who will be a loyal member of the workforce but this doesn't mean that you cannot have your own opinions and preferences. If you disagree with something, say so in a polite, assertive manner. You needn't be aggressive. Many interviewers do everything they can to make the interview appear like a 'natural' conversation. Even so, at times there may be a period of silence. Don't let it worry you. He is probably thinking of his next question or trying to take in all the information you are giving him. Remember also that an interviewer may be as nervous as you are. You can both have temporary lapses of memory. He may struggle to recall the next question and likewise you may completely forget how to respond to a particular line of his enquiry. It is natural and it can happen to anyone – tell him your mind has gone blank and ask if you can move on to the next question.

If you have prepared yourself well, nervousness shouldn't be a major problem, but there are a couple of things to watch out for. Give the interviewer time to finish his question before you start to answer it and make sure that you listen hard to the question. In your preparation you will have rehearsed several answers to a number of imaginary questions, but this question will not be identical to one of those which you imagined so you must tailor your response to suit the particular question. A stock, off-the-peg, response won't do.

Try to take evidence of your work to the interview. If you are applying for a clerical job, you could put together a portfolio of examples of your work on a word processor. If the job demands design or artistic skill you may have a portfolio or examples of projects carried out in your current employment, school or college. Trade and craft workers can often impress interviewers by producing photographs of their work.

Throughout the interview you can monitor your performance by keeping a close eye on the interviewer's body language. If he is looking at you or nodding his head, he is attentive and encouraging you to say more. An interviewer who is tapping his watch or glancing at the clock on the wall is inadvertently telling you that you have lost his interest or that your answer is too lengthy.

Always try to present a positive attitude. Mention positive aspects of previous jobs and do not criticise previous employers. It comes across as disloyalty.

Don't smoke during an interview, even if you are offered a cigarette, and don't chew gum. You may be offered a cup of coffee but it is often better to refuse politely. You need to concentrate on answering the questions well and making sure that your message is getting across, a cup of coffee can be distracting and it can cramp your style. If you are nervous, a cup and saucer in your hand can magnify even the tiniest of tremors.

Towards the end of the interview most interviewers will ask if you have any questions. If you discover that the questions you intended to ask have been answered during the course of your conversation, tell the interviewer that your questions have all been answered and then say: 'But I'm very interested in this job so if I do think of anything during the next few days would you mind if I telephoned you?' In that way you are letting him know how keen you are and you're also keeping the door open for the future.

Finally, at the end of the interview be sure to thank the interviewer for his time and interest in you, maintain your composure until you leave the building and then, once outside, analyse your thoughts and feelings before you lose touch with them.

- What questions were you asked?
- What aspects of the interview went well?
- Were there any difficult questions?
- What would you do differently next time?
- What aspects of your performance do you need to work on?

You'll be lucky if you get the first job you apply for. Most people don't manage it but, if you use it as a learning experience, you never 'fail'. You come away knowing more about interview technique and you can use the experience to improve your performance the next time.

Some interviewers offer 'feedback' to unsuccessful candidates. They are willing to talk to you after the event to point out the positive and negative sides of your performance. If it's offered, take the opportunity – it can only serve to help you prepare for the next job application. Remember, too, that you may be more experienced than your interviewer. Whatever the result, you emerge from the interview richer in experience and more highly skilled. If he can't recognise talent when he sees it, he's the loser – not you!

Further information

Great Answers to Tough Interview Questions, 3rd edition, Martin John Yate (Kogan Page, 1992)

Successful Interview Skills, Rebecca Corfield (Kogan Page, 1992)

Test Your Own Aptitude, 2nd edition, J Barrett and G Williams (Kogan Page, 1990)

Interviewers *See* Interviews

Most managers agree that the ability to interview candidates well is a prime management skill. An organisation's strength depends on the quality of its workforce, so a manager's decision about your ability to do the job is one of the most important he ever takes. In this sense the interview is as important to the interviewer as to the interviewee. Selecting the wrong person for a job can be a long-term black mark on a manager's record sheet.

Some interviewers are highly skilled. They have been well trained and have had a great deal of experience in obtaining the information they require in order to make a rational judgement about a candidate's job suitability.

Good interviewers are methodical, they do their homework and they ensure that there is a structure to the questions they ask. They know what skills and qualities they are looking for and they make sure that they have all the information they need to make a sound decision before the candidate leaves the room. No matter how relaxed and natural the experience may seem, a good interviewer will ensure that the discussion progresses logically covering all the job requirements.

Many interviewers like to begin with a simple 'icebreaker' question designed to establish a relationship and set you at ease. 'Tell me, Mr Robinson, what particularly attracts you to this line of work?', or 'Could you tell me briefly a little about yourself and why you have applied for this job?'

Next, they may wish to ask questions about your background and your experience in previous jobs. The next cluster of questions may seek to explore your range of skills and then they may move on to test your temperament for the job. Different interviewers take different approaches. Some may prefer to cluster their questions around headings such as leadership ability, communication skill, planning ability, motivation and technical knowledge. If one question doesn't produce the required information an interviewer will come back to the matter with another question – from a different angle, perhaps.

Interviewers sometimes like to move from theoretical questions to practical questions and back again. They ask questions about hypothetical situations and then request practical examples of how you have dealt with similar situations in the past. Good interviewers are also able to move from general questions, 'What would you do if . . .?', to specific ones, 'When did you last use a piece of machinery such as this?', or 'What was the size of budget you were responsible for in your last job?' Sound theoretical knowledge added to successful past experience counts for much in many interviewers' eyes.

The information which interviewers look for may sometimes be simple and factual requiring a short yes or no answer. 'Do you have a clean driving licence?', for example; but other information may be harder to obtain, in which case the interviewer will switch to open questions which encourage you to talk about a subject at greater length. Such questions often begin with, 'How do you feel about . . .?' or 'What do you think about . . .?'

Although some managers are excellent interviewers, there is an equally large number of poor ones. They may have had little or no training and be somewhat inexperienced. Some interviewers will be as nervous as you. They may not have interviewed anyone for several years and so, if you want the job, you'll have to set them at ease. Be polite, smile and use your body language to let them know that you are calm and friendly. Some poor interviewers will have trouble finding questions to ask. They will want you to talk to them but, through lack of training, they will inadvertently pose questions which require little more than a one- or two-word response.

'You know how to drive a car, don't you?'
'Yes, I do.'
'Do you like driving?'
'Yes.'

In such a situation, you'll need to see beyond the interviewer's question. In this case he probably wants to get to know you, discover where your interest in driving comes from, and find out what experience you've had. Unfortunately, any question beginning with the word 'Do' can be answered with a simple 'Yes' or 'No'. You'll have to do the work for him and enlarge on your response to give him the information you think he wants rather than the information he appears to have asked for.

There are jobs which are highly stressful, in which case it is legitimate for interviewers deliberately to create a stressful situation in order to see how you handle it. There are interviewers, however, who seem to feel that an interview is an intellectual point-scoring exercise. Many good interviewers may challenge a statement you make during your interview to see how you respond, but poor interviewers seem to feel that it is their job to challenge every general statement you make in order to prove something about themselves to you. There are no easy answers here. Such people are out of their depth, and when you know that, you can smile inwardly and keep your dignity. Roll with the punches, stay calm, speak slowly, deliberately and clearly. When you walk away unruffled think long and hard about whether you want to work for someone as inadequate at that.

Interviews *See* Interviewers

The purpose of an interview is for the employer to get to know the person behind the application form and see how his approach will fit in with the company's style. No two interviews are the same, different organisations have different methods and procedures. Some have no methods at all.

Before the formal selection interview, some organisations use pre-liminary interviews to 'screen out' unlikely candidates and achieve a briefer, more manageable shortlist. These interviews may be carried out by individual managers or personnel staff. Sometimes the screening-out interview is done by telephone. From the employer's point of view, a telephone discussion with a candidate saves time and is considerably cheaper than a face-to-face meeting.

Telephone interviews are not easy. The interviewer doesn't have much evidence on which to make his judgement. He cannot judge your suitability for a post by reading the many signals you would give him were you sitting across the table in the interview room. He cannot see how you present yourself and therefore his judgement is based purely on the sound of your voice, how you respond to questions, your tone, intonation and use of language. From your point of view, it can be difficult to impress an interviewer who cannot see you, so you need to work hard at sounding 'likeable'. If possible try to ensure that your telephone interview takes place in a location where you can be relaxed and undisturbed. If you are in an office ask someone to guard the door for you and divert calls away from other telephones on desks close by. If you are at home, ensure that children or other members of the family are warned not to interrupt you. In your discussion, even though you cannot be seen, try to smile. It can make you sound more assertive and friendly.

Having determined a shortlist, companies have a variety of interview options available to them. Broadly speaking, however, their approach will be based on a selection from three possibilities.

The simplest selection interview, often favoured by small companies, will be the one-to-one meeting between you and the interviewer. He may be a manager, the owner of the company or a recruitment specialist acting on behalf of the employer. When they work out well these interviews are the closest thing to a natural conversation. They can be pleasant, relaxed affairs. They can go badly wrong, however, if the interviewer takes a dislike to you. Clearly, with only one person making the decision, one-to-one interviews can be biased in favour of a particular type of person. In such an interview, you may find yourself having to contend with one person's idiosyncratic views about what makes an ideal candidate. At such times, stay calm and friendly – don't be tempted to argue or flounce out of the room. Often interviewers belong to the same professional group or social club – don't give anyone an 'awful interview' anecdote they can tell against you. In a one-to-one interview you may have to accept that the best candidate for a job may be overlooked in favour of one who more closely mirrors the interviewer's bias.

'Panel' interviews, where you will be faced by a number of interviewers asking their questions in turn, are favoured by some companies. The composition and size of an interview panel varies. Local authorities, for example, may include councillors on their interview panel. Some panels ask each candidate exactly the same questions, others prepare different questions for each candidate. Some organisations set up interviews as simple question and answer sessions but others may expect you to prepare a presentation.

Panel interviewing is popular because it reduces the possibility of personal idiosyncrasies clouding the decision. Supporters of the panel interview argue that it enables an organisation to gain a broader insight into a candidate and take a more comprehensive view of his suitability for the post.

Arranging a panel interview involves the co-ordination of busy diaries, so it is customary for interview panels to see shortlisted candidates in turn, making the decision about who will be offered the job at the end of the session when the last candidate has been seen. Panel interviews can be fairer than one-to-one interviews but they can also be more stressful.

Many organisations use a 'sequence' of separate interviews to arrive at their final choice of candidate. Sequential interviewing enables an employer to expose you to a wide range of interviewers who may use each interview to concentrate on particular aspects of the job or particular qualities which will be required of the successful candidate. This enables companies to gain a great deal of knowledge about you and it ensures that the final decision is made in the light of a wide range of opinion.

When recruiting to sensitive or senior level posts, some organisations use sequential interviews as part of a much more sophisticated recruitment process known as an 'assessment centre'. It is a term which can be confusing in that it applies to a 'process' of testing rather than the geographical location where it takes place. Assessment centres were first used by the allied forces during the Second World War as a means of selecting the most appropriate personnel for specific military responsibilities.

All jobs require a range of skills and qualities. Sometimes these are referred to as 'competencies'. In an assessment centre, candidates are put through a series of tests, simulations, exercises and interviews specifically designed to test them against a checklist of competencies which are known to be relevant to this particular job. The basic idea of an assessment centre is to collect as much information as possible about a candidate using the widest range of evidence. Trained assessors then use that information to make judgements about each candidate's strengths and weaknesses in different areas relevant to the job.

An assessment centre can often take two days to complete and it may involve physical tests as well as group work, role-play exercises and psychological assessments. In an assessment centre candidates are observed at all times. Even when the formal tests are over and candidates are relaxing in the evening, company executives may be present to see who makes friends easily, who retreats behind a newspaper, and even who has one drink too many. Within an assessment centre, the interview is seen as part of a much wider selection process. Performance at interview is only one of a variety of measures used to enable a selection panel to make its decision.

Further information
Interviews Made Easy, Mark Parkinson (Kogan Page, 1994)

Successful Interview Skills, Rebecca Corfield (Kogan Page, 1992)

Winning at your Interview, Michael Stevens (Kogan Page, 1990)

J

Jobcentre

Jobcentres offer a free service to employers who phone in and give details of their vacancies. On receipt of the information Jobcentre staff complete advertisement cards and mount them on display. So, on the face of it, the local Jobcentre seems like an obvious first port of call for anyone looking for a job. To use Jobcentres well, however, you need to know a little more about their strengths and limitations. Some employers always contact the Jobcentre when they have a vacancy. As it's free they may choose not to advertise anywhere else. In effect, if you don't visit the Jobcentre you may never know about some vacancies.

Some companies never contact Jobcentres at all. So no matter how many jobs are displayed, you can be confident that you haven't got the full picture if you restrict your jobhunting to chasing Jobcentre opportunities. You should always look elsewhere too. To get the best from a Jobcentre you need to visit every day. If you don't, by the time you see a vacancy on the noticeboard, it could have been seen by hundreds of other jobhunters.

In addition to advertising jobs, the Jobcentre is often the local base for the current government initiative to help unemployed people. Government initiatives are not always well publicised and their emphasis can change quickly, but they are designed to help you so you may as well take advantage of them.

Jobcentre staff usually offer good advice about support and assistance for jobhunters and they can often give you useful background information on jobs advertised by them. When you decide to follow up a Jobcentre lead, the Jobcentre staff may telephone the company to arrange an interview for you. If you decide to telephone the company and introduce yourself, prepare carefully what you are going to say. Try something like – 'Hello, my name is Pat Smith, I'm phoning about the job advertised in the Jobcentre.' Never begin your conversation by saying, 'The people at the Jobcentre said I should phone you.'

Jobclub

Jobclubs are funded by the government and are usually closely linked to local **Jobcentres**. In a jobclub you can expect to find a wide range of directories to help you identify companies which employ people with your skills. They often provide paper, envelopes and stamps free of charge, and they offer training in all aspects of jobhunting. At a jobclub, you can obtain help with writing **letters of application** and **CVs** or you can be given help in developing your **interview technique**. Jobclubs are one of a number of **support groups** which offer valuable support to jobhunters.

Job description

A good job description should begin with a job title and the title of the person who will be your boss. It should also describe where this job fits into the hierarchy of the organisation. In large organisations it may tell you the 'grade' of the post, and the section or department you will be working in. In one or two simple sentences, it should tell you the purpose of the job. For example: 'To administer the company pension scheme, ensuring the collection of all contributions and the prompt and accurate payment of benefits.'

Then the job description should list those things for which you will be accountable. This should not be a simple list of tasks. Keeping your boss's diary, for example, is a 'task' which shouldn't be listed on a job description. Technology may change and the diary may be thrown in the wastebin in favour of a new computer system. You will still remain responsible for keeping his appointments but the 'task' of keeping a diary will be obsolete. A good job description should have longer-term value. It may say: 'Provide administrative support to the manager – filing, arranging meetings and appointments, and assisting with correspondence.'

There may be nine or ten 'accountabilities' listed on the job description and a few brief paragraphs about the knowledge and experience required to do the job properly.

If you are sent a good job description, read it carefully. In your letter of application you can point out that you have the skills required to take on the responsibilities listed. At interview, you will probably be asked questions to test your ability and your attitude against each of the accountabilities mentioned. Use the job description to think of questions you may be asked about each of these aspects of the job and then try to come up with a good answer. Think about previous experiences which you can use to illustrate your competence to take on these responsibilities. You won't predict the exact words of the questions you will be asked at interview but you'll be close.

JOB DESCRIPTION

Most people are stronger in some areas than others but remember that enthusiasm can be used to offset deficiencies in skill. Perhaps you aren't an expert in every aspect of the job but you can tell the interviewer that you are keen and eager to learn.

With practice, you can spot a good job description and make use of it in your application for a job. If you are faced with a poor one, you may need to spend some time reading between the lines.

K

Knowledge and experience required

Employers often use a particular code when they describe the knowledge and experience required by someone doing a particular job. Skills which a person should have on the first day of work will be described as 'required' or 'essential'. Less important knowledge and experience will be described as 'desirable'.

Knowledge and experience
A reasonable standard of general education and accuracy with figures are essential. A methodical mind and an ability to communicate verbally and in writing are also required. Previous experience in the pensions department of a large organisation is also desirable.

If you have the 'essential' skills, don't worry too much about the rest – just make a good application and see what happens. You might be pleasantly surprised. You may never have worked in a pensions department before but you know that they will ask you what previous relevant experience you have had, so you have plenty of time to think about similar experiences. Perhaps you worked in the accounts department of a large company for a couple of years. You didn't handle the pensions side of the work but the experience was similar enough to be relevant.

When you are thinking of making an application, look at the knowledge and experience required and see how your background, experience and temperament meet the requirements. Try to look at the information in a positive way and count the number of points in your favour. Don't worry too much about the knowledge and skill which you do not have. If they want you badly enough, they may be prepared to offer you the job, train you and bring you up to speed.

L

Labour market information

When you are looking for a job you need to know what kind of people employers are seeking to recruit. Some areas of the country may have a surplus of people with skills similar to yours but other places may be desperate to recruit you. If you are thinking of changing your career or investing in a training course, it is even more important that you try to get a sound and accurate picture of what is happening in the market-place and how things may change in the future. Predicting employment trends is not an exact science but there are a number of sources of information.

If you are under 21, or have left full-time further education within the last two years, careers officers may be able to offer you advice. They will be able to suggest openings for people with your skills and qualifications. Careers officers are in constant touch with a wide range of employers so they are able to gain a good local view of employment trends. They will know which companies are growing and which are standing still. They should be able to tell you which kinds of job are regularly advertised and the areas of work which are shrinking. If you are over 21, **Jobcentre** staff should be able to offer a similar overview.

You could also carry out your own survey. Read the national press every day for a month to spot employment trends and, during the same period, check out the local press every evening. What kinds of job are advertised the most? What new developments have been reported locally? You could use the Yellow Pages to telephone companies which employ people with the skills you have, or hope to get, and ask whether they envisage taking on new staff within the foreseeable future. Who knows? One company may be just about to place an advertisement!

Training and Enterprise Councils (TECs) and Local Enterprise Companies (LECs) in Scotland are responsible for putting money and resources into further education and training in each area. They also fund training schemes. The decision about how much to invest in training for different types of work is often based on forecasts about how many jobs there are likely to be in your area in the foreseeable future. Give your TEC or LEC a call; staff there may be able to give you a broad picture of future trends locally. Your local TEC may also be able to advise you of any special support it is able to arrange if you have been unemployed for a long time.

Large organisations

Large organisations usually have set procedures for most things. When it comes to recruiting staff they often have a team of trained personnel officers who handle the whole recruitment process on behalf of the various departments and sections.

If you are applying for a job in a large organisation you will probably be expected to respond to an advertisement by telephoning and asking for further details and an application form. Usually you'll receive general information about the organisation and more specific information about the job which is available. You are often given about two weeks to make your application.

If you are shortlisted you can be almost certain that references will be taken up and that you will be interviewed by more than one person. Applying for a job in a large organisation can seem quite threatening. Letters sent to you will be formal and businesslike, you may be asked to undergo entrance examinations and health checks, and the whole process may seem impersonal and bound by procedure. But there is a positive side to the process – most of the books written about jobhunting seem to be based on experience gained in large organisations. Their advice concerning letters of application, CVs and interview technique is particularly sound and relevant to the recruitment processes you will encounter when you apply for such jobs. So the experience should be fairly predictable and there is a wealth of good advice available.

Late applications

When a vacancy is advertised, most companies give applicants about two weeks to complete and return their forms. Often the closing date for applications will be mentioned in the advertisement or in the further details sent to people who express an interest in the post.

When you apply for a job, you must do everything you can to ensure that your application arrives on time but, if you cannot meet the deadline, take a close look at the closing date. Friday is a popular day for closing recruitment to a job. It allows a manager to take applications home over the weekend so that he can study them in relative peace and quiet. It also allows for a few late applications to arrive over the weekend. So, if necessary, you can get a late application in without too much trouble. As long as you have the application forms by the end of the working day on the Friday deadline you can spend Saturday completing the forms and drop them into the company's letterbox by hand on the Sunday. Your application will be late but not late enough to ruin your chances.

Once a job has closed things begin to move apace and shortlisting takes place fairly quickly. If you suspect that your application may arrive after the deadline phone the company and warn staff that it is on its way. Make sure you have a good reason for your application being late.

Leisure learning

Leisure learning classes take place in a variety of locations. Some are based in colleges, others in local schools and community centres. They can be a key factor in getting a job. Don't be put off by the traditional view of evening classes as nothing more than 'macramé' or 'machine knitting'!

Throughout July and August a wide variety of colleges and other institutions advertise their programmes of classes and courses which begin in the following September. Many are recreational but a significant number are of interest to anyone wanting to build on their range of workplace skills. A few years ago Computer Studies was a favourite course. Our understanding of technology has since developed and you are now more likely to find courses dealing with specific applications and types of software. Many typing classes have also been replaced by courses in word processing, usually leading to RSA qualifications. Some course programmes also offer shorthand or speedwriting. Tuition in languages is another major area of activity and many organisers try to ensure that they are able to offer a reasonable range of GCSE and A level subjects.

Most courses have to cover the cost of tuition out of enrolment fees, so every effort is made to ensure that they take place in locations and at times convenient to the maximum number of people. For this reason the largest part of a local course programme will be scheduled to take place between 7 and 9 pm on Monday to Thursday evenings. As well as the planned annual course programme, there may also be short one- or two-day 'taster' classes which often take place at weekends.

If you are out of a paid job short part-time courses can offer a lifeline. The support you receive from others in the same predicament can be a significant factor in helping you through your difficulties. Many centres offer reduced rates for people who are not in receipt of a wage.

If you are in work, courses can help you to update your skills and cope with changes in technology. Let your boss know that you are attending evening classes to increase your work-related skills – he'll probably be impressed. Who knows? He may even contribute towards the cost of the enrolment fee.

To discover the range of courses available in your area get prospectuses or leaflets from your local college; keep an eye on the local newspaper for advertisements of new classes and look out for course information displayed in your local library. See also **Mature entry**.

Letters of application

When they have a vacancy, some employers send out application forms but others expect candidates to write a letter of application.

Most people enclose a **curriculum vitae** with a letter of application. This is a simple catalogue of basic information about you. It gives your name, address, and information about your educational background and qualifications, your employment history, and your hobbies and interests. With a CV, your letter of application can be kept short but it must be written with care and, if you want to have any chance of getting an interview, it should be written for a specific job. A general letter enquiring about possible vacancies will not do. Don't worry, though; letters of application often follow a set formula and they get easier to write as you get more practice.

Essentially, a letter of application is a business letter. If possible, it should be typed or produced on a word processor but if you cannot get access to either a typewriter or a word processor, a handwritten version will be just as effective, provided that it is neat and without spelling mistakes. If you choose the handwritten option use black ink – it's easier to photocopy.

Whatever technology you decide on, your letter should be written on plain A4 paper. Put your address, telephone number and the date at the top right-hand corner of the page and begin your letter underneath. If you know the name of the manager of the company you can address him by name, 'Dear Mr Smith,' – but check the spelling first. Alternatively, 'Dear Sir,' will do just as well. If you intend to enclose a CV, you can produce an effective letter of application in five short paragraphs.

Your first paragraph should state clearly the name of the job you are seeking and where you saw it advertised. Bear in mind that companies are frequently seeking to fill more than one job so make it clear which one you are applying for. Your second paragraph should make a general statement about why you are applying for the job. Perhaps you have extensive experience in this kind of job or you have always

LETTERS OF APPLICATION

49 Elmwood Drive
Town View Estate
Manchester M17 2NE
Tel (072) 509 53504

19 June 19XX

Mr K Smith
Personnel Officer
North West Components Ltd
212–214 West Way
Stanley Industrial Estate
Manchester M19 3NW

Dear Mr Smith

I am writing to enquire about the possibility of obtaining clerical
work within your organisation. I am twenty-seven years old and
I have a four year old child who is now happily placed in a local
nursery.

As you will see from the enclosed CV, I have had five years'
experience of clerical work in the offices of Brown and Co,
a company I joined on completion of my full-time training at
Manchester College of Further Education.

Having taken time out in order to raise a family, I am eager
return to full-time employment and I would greatly appreciate
any opportunity of joining the staff of North West Components
Ltd. I believe my references will confirm that I am hard working,
highly motivated, and career minded.

I should be grateful if you could contact me should there be any
vacancies within your company which might suit my background
and experience. Please also keep my information on file in case
of future openings.

Thank you for your attention in this matter. I enclosed a stamped
addressed envelope for your reply.

Yours sincerely

Nicola Winters

23 Norwood Crescent
The Oaks
Plymouth
PM1 6TX

1 December 19XX

Dear Sir

I should like to apply for the post of Training Officer which was advertised in the *Plymouth Echo* yesterday evening. My curriculum vitae is enclosed.

I have had a great deal of experience in training and staff development at all levels within organisations. I believe training is an important means by which an organisation can achieve its objectives and, in view of this, I have always taken every opportunity to develop my skills and further my knowledge in this area.

Currently I am employed as the administration manager in the southern branch offices of Dalton Freight Ltd, where all types of haulage services are provided to UK and Continental customers. In this role I am responsible for ensuring a smooth and effective administrative service to fifteen managers and area representatives who act on behalf of over one thousand customers in the southern region of the UK and northern France. I am directly responsible for managing the work of seven accounts clerks, thirteen word processor operators and four secretaries/receptionists.

The recent opening of the single market and frequent changes in EC directives regarding transport and freight movement to and from the UK have presented great challenges and opportunities to all companies in this field. One of my roles within the company is to ensure that all administrative staff receive appropriate and timely training to ensure their continued effectiveness during a period of great change. In this respect, I believe that training has been a major contributor to this company's recent success in attracting increased orders during a recession.

Throughout my career I have used training as a means of encouraging initiative and motivation among staff. Four years ago, while working at Dury and Young Ltd, I took responsibility for the induction of new staff and the overseeing of YTS trainees within the company. Before that, while working in Hylton Construction Ltd, I was responsible for the production of the company health and safety policy and all the staff training which ensued. Today, my interest in training has led me to develop opportunities for administrative staff to gain vocational qualifications through NVQ awards. To this end, I have recently qualified as an NVQ skills assessor.

In my career to date, I have been responsible for the management and training of a wide range of staff. I am able to contribute to the development of ability at all levels within an organisation and I have a proven track record in the design and delivery of training packages. As someone who is highly motivated and commercially minded, I view this post as an exciting opportunity to focus my skills and contribute to the continued work of your company at a time of great change and development. I should be most grateful to be considered suitable for interview.

Yours faithfully

S Jones

wanted the chance to do this type of work. Perhaps you've just obtained your qualifications and you see this as an important first step on the career ladder. Either way, keep it short but make sure that your suitability for the post is well understood.

You can now use a paragraph to give the employer more information about yourself and why he should be interested in you for this particular job. This paragraph could describe your present job and encourage him to believe that the job he has to offer is a logical career move for you. You could let him know that you are ready to take on this new challenge, or you could highlight the skills and qualities required of you in your present job and show how these would be useful for anyone taking on the tasks he needs done. Here you could also refer to your enclosed CV and mention one or two previous jobs in which you successfully undertook similar work or carried similar levels of responsibility.

In paragraph four you could write about the type of person you are. You could stress that your background and temperament are ideal for the type of work you seek and you could illustrate your commitment to the work by mentioning qualifications you have obtained, training courses you have attended or particular achievements, in or out of work, which you think indicate your strengths and qualities.

Finally, finish with a strong statement about how much you would value working for this organisation and tell the reader that you would welcome the opportunity of an interview.

If you are straight out of school or college, you can't show a long employment history but you should be able to explain why the courses you have studied are relevant to the job you are applying for. You can also tell the employer about the range of tools and equipment you are familiar with – photocopiers and personal computers, for example. Perhaps you know how to drive too. Highlight one or two areas of study which particularly interested you and remember to mention any work-experience placements you've had and how much you enjoyed them.

When you have finished and checked every word, sign the letter and take a photocopy. Every letter of application has to be different because you are applying for different jobs but there is always something which you can steal from the last letter you wrote – so if you write a good one, be sure to keep a copy. Finally, address the envelope correctly, and get it into the post box well before the closing date for applications.

Libraries

These are the jobhunter's most valuable resource. In the reference library you will find trade directories which will list companies, their activities and their interests. You can use them to compile lists of organisations you intend to target in your job search or to gain useful information about a company before you write you application. Many libraries also hold telephone directories and Yellow Pages which give you access to addresses and telephone numbers of companies nation-wide. *British Rate and Data* will give you the names and addresses of trade magazines which may carry advertisements for the type of work you seek or, alternatively, you may decide to use it to discover a suitable publication in which to place an ad of your own. Libraries also carry copies of local, regional and national newspapers so you can scan the columns every day for free. They also have photocopying facilities and the interloan service enables you to order specialist books to keep you up to date in the area of work where you are hoping to get a job. Above all, libraries are warm, dry and quiet – perfect places for making an application without the constant distractions you get at home.

Lifelong learning

'Lifelong learning' and 'continuing education' are phrases used by educationalists to describe the urgent need for all of us to accept the fact that learning is a continuous lifelong process. It doesn't end when we leave school. Education, training and retraining are going to be increasingly important aspects of our lives and in the future we will be expected to take much more responsibility for our own development both in and out of work. Today there are more learning options available than ever before and a much greater choice of routes to qualifications.

Learning is a key factor in gaining and holding a job but, with such a wide variety of options available, you will need to do your homework carefully to make sure that you get the best out of what is available. Read prospectuses or leaflets about courses from your local college; keep an eye on the local paper for advertisements for new courses, and check out information displayed in the public library about learning opportunities. Local colleges should also be able to tell you about new ways of gaining qualifications through **National Vocational Qualifications** and **accreditation of prior learning**.

Think also about **distance learning** options and routes into **higher education** for mature students. If you are unemployed, your local **Jobcentre** should also be able to let you know of current government training initiatives. When it comes to getting a job, if you can show that you are interested and keen to learn, you are half way there.

In areas of high unemployment some local education authorities believe that education is an important contributor to local economic development. Course organisers take the view that companies will not invest in a region unless there is a skilled, articulate and motivated workforce in the area ready to take on the jobs which are to be created. As a result, in some parts of the country there are day-time classes, clubs and support groups for people who are out of work. Often a crèche is provided so that parents of small children can get some free time to study or make job applications. Staff and volunteers are also able to offer advice and help when it comes to writing letters of application, preparing curricula vitae and completing application forms. They also offer support in adult literacy and numeracy. Organisers are keen to respond to local demand so if you don't see what you are looking for, make contact and have a word. You'll be surprised what can be achieved. Details of clubs and day-time classes can be found in public libraries. Alternatively, phone your local education authority.

Local Enterprise Companies see *Training and Enterprise Councils*

Local press

The local newspaper and the freesheets which are pushed through your door each week can provide you with a rich source of information. Their emphasis on neighbourhood news makes them particularly useful to anyone who is only able to seek work within a particular geographical area. Obviously, the job advertisements are the first items to look at in a local paper, but don't stop there. Read all the news and feature articles and look out for snippets of information which tell you about the local employment scene.

- Is any company launching a new product?
- Has any local firm attracted an unusually large order?
- Are any new companies moving into the area?
- Are there any new shops opening in the town centre?

Any information like this could be significant. Perhaps you should write a speculative letter to these companies enquiring about possible job opportunities.

A few years ago, a young man noticed that a local company had placed an advertisement for a senior member of staff in the local newspaper. He didn't have the right background or experience for the job but the advertisement stated that the vacancy had arisen owing to company plans for expansion. He wrote a speculative letter of application explaining that he would be grateful to be considered for any post which might arise as a result of the planned expansion. He was contacted a few months later and, following an interview, was offered a job with the company.

M

Mature entry

Some companies have positive views about employing mature people. They feel that, on the whole, people with a wide experience of life score more highly in the workplace than younger people who, on paper at least, may seem better qualified. Don't let lack of formal qualifications put you off either. Many colleges and professional bodies have special arrangements for recognising the potential of people who don't have the qualifications you would expect of those about to leave full-time education.

If you are considering starting afresh in a new career, make sure that you will enjoy a reasonable length of time in your new occupation before you reach the upper age limit. Forty years old, for example, is not the best time to begin training as a PE teacher. The best advice is to find out as much as you can about the nature of the work and the job opportunities before you commit yourself to retraining. While some companies actively encourage mature jobhunters, others are tied to insurance companies who discourage the employment of people over a certain age. **Jobcentres** and **recruitment agencies** are usually aware of careers and companies where upper age limits apply.

Money

Lovely, isn't it! And most of us could make use of a little bit more. Getting a job is about earning money. After all, if you have worked hard you deserve the rewards. Money means that you can pay your bills, buy a car, save towards a holiday, or move into a new house or flat. Money gives you a degree of freedom and a sense of worth. If you are earning money you can stand on your own two feet and no one can push you around. Well, that's largely true but it's not the whole picture.

If you are young, you will find that the jobs which pay the most are the ones which offer the poorest long-term gain. Jobs which offer sound training and day-release opportunities pay much less but, when you qualify, the tables are turned and your earnings soon overtake those of your friends who chased the fat wage earlier on. It may take three or four years for that to happen and at 16 that can seem a long time. Remember, though, that you will probably have a working life of at least 40 years. As a qualified and skilled worker you have a career ahead of you, but without training and qualifications you may not even have a job for long.

At 16 you may have had enough of school and be eager to gain independence. A highly paid job, if you can find one, may seem an attractive proposition. Think about it carefully, though, and talk it through with as many people as you want to. Careers teachers will probably advise you to think about further education or a job with training. Failing that, they may suggest a **Youth Training** placement. In every case, they should be prepared to take some time and help you to arrive at your decision.

Mature people often face the same dilemma. They take a job simply because of the higher wage and often regret their decision almost immediately. The new job may require them to work difficult shifts, the work may be too pressured or the distances they have to travel too great. It's great to get a job that you really wanted and, if it pays more than you are earning now, that's a bonus, but money is only a short-term motivator. If you've taken a job that you have no interest in simply for the money, you'll probably want to leave within a couple of months.

Morale

You can spend months or even years waiting for the right job to come your way, and when you think of the number of applicants there are for some particularly attractive jobs, it can be hard to imagine that you will ever be the successful candidate. At times like these it can be difficult to keep up your morale, especially if you've tried for half a dozen jobs and got nowhere. Remember that getting a job can change your life overnight. One day, you can feel a million miles from your target and yet, the next day, a successful interview can give you everything you've always wanted.

When times are hard and all your friends seem to be successful in their jobs, it pays to remember that your time will come – provided you are doing everything right. If the work you seek is appropriate to your background and skill, if you are careful in writing your letters of application and if your CV is well designed and accurate, you will certainly be making a better application than most. If you are regularly invited for interview, you are already streets ahead of your rivals and you are a serious contender for the posts you apply for. Use each interview as a piece of action research and learn from it. Even an interview which doesn't lead to an offer of a job can be a positive experience.

Finally, bear in mind that it only takes an employer two or three minutes to shake your hand and offer you a job. Your situation could be radically different this time next week. By then, you may have forgotten why you felt so low.

Motivation

When you are looking for a job, you are your own boss. You need to be a self-starter. No one is going to ask you to fill in an application form or telephone a list of employers to see if any are looking for extra staff. No one will search the newspaper ads for you and only you can write your own CV. The motivation to find a new job must come from you, and it is important that you know why you are doing this. There may be a few disappointments in store for you along the jobhunting road but if you know what you want, and if you want it badly enough, you won't be tempted to give up.

People often get jobs simply because they won't give up. Other people who may be better qualified and experienced often don't have the staying power to keep applying. The definition of a professional writer is 'an amateur who wouldn't quit'; you can apply this to most walks of life. Keep making applications and use every experience to gain a little more knowledge of the jobhunting game. Many people who now hold senior positions in companies aren't particularly skilled or gifted – they are just more persistent.

N

National press

Some national newspapers run advertisements for particular types of job on different days of the week. On Mondays, for example, the *Guardian* publishes advertisements of vacancies in creative occupations, the media, marketing and secretarial work. On Tuesdays it publishes educational vacancies. On Wednesdays it concentrates on public appointments. On Thursdays it runs commercial job ads and on Fridays it covers the environment and housing sectors.

The Times covers secretarial and education areas each Monday, legal appointments on Tuesdays, and media and marketing on Wednesdays. Public appointments along with information technology, accounting and engineering posts are advertised each Thursday.

Other newspapers prefer to put all their job ads together on the same day. The *Daily Mail*, for example, publishes the bulk of its job ads each Thursday.

It is worthwhile making sure that you see each newspaper regularly on the appropriate days. The prices of some have fallen recently and anyway, with luck, you will only need to buy one paper each day. Alternatively, use your regular visits to the public library to monitor them all. Libraries often carry copies of several daily newspapers.

National Vocational Qualification

NVQs are qualifications which recognise and give you credit for workplace skills. They are awarded at different levels to reflect the degree of skill required in different types of job. NVQ level 2 is regarded as roughly the equivalent of four good GCSEs. NVQ level 3 carries the same weight as a couple of A levels.

If you worked in an office you might be expected to operate a word processor and use a range of software packages. You might also be expected to use a photocopier, a paper trimmer, a telephone and a fax machine. There are a number of aspects to every job and a wide range of tasks which have to be performed. NVQs break down all the aspects of a type of job and call them 'units'. Each unit is composed of a number of 'elements' which describe the level and the range of skills that a 'competent' worker in that job would be expected to have. NVQs are not courses of study; they are simple statements about what people should be able to do in the workplace. You may find that you have already been working at a particular level. In an office, for example, if you regularly use a photocopier, a fax machine and a word processor, you are probably already well down the road to achieving an NVQ qualification. All you need to do is gather the evidence and convince your boss that it is a good idea to let you be assessed.

With NVQs there are no examinations to sit. You work towards gaining an NVQ certificate by proving your ability to carry out aspects of the job described in each unit. You can show that you are competent to carry out tasks at the required level by demonstrating your ability to an NVQ assessor. Through discussion with him and by collecting a portfolio of 'evidence', you gain NVQ credits for each unit of competence which you obtain and you can work at your own pace.

NVQs are attractive qualifications. They don't test your knowledge of theory or your ability to write long essays. They measure what you can do in the workplace and they give you credit for that. More information about NVQs can be obtained from colleges of further education, the careers service or your local **Training and Enterprise Council**. Alternatively, contact the National Council for Vocational Qualifications and ask what NVQs have been developed for your field of work.

Further information
The National Council for Vocational Qualifications, 222 Euston Road, London NW1 2BZ; 0171-387 9898

Networking

When you are looking for a job you need information. Friends and contacts provide one of the most effective ways of getting it. The more people you talk to, the better informed you will be. If you are unemployed, it does no harm to let people know that you are looking for work. They may know of interesting leads for you to follow or be able to put you in touch with other people who can offer help and advice. Spread your net far and wide; the more people who know about you the better.

If you are currently in employment but looking for a better job, you will still benefit from having a strong network but you may need to be a little more subtle. You may not want people to know that you are hoping to move on. Talk to friends and colleagues about work, new developments, trends and initiatives. Show a genuine interest in work-related topics and you'll be surprised what you can learn about job opportunities in your particular field. You needn't mention that you may be a candidate.

Finally, bear in mind that many professional bodies have magazines with job vacancies. Some professional associations are also able to offer advice on entry and training opportunities. Many such organisations have special rates for students who wish to join. Professional organisations are listed in *British Qualifications*, published annually by Kogan Page.

O

On your bike!

Not everyone is free to move around the country in search of employment but if you are able to travel it is worth bearing in mind that the type of job you seek may be available elsewhere in the country. Many people with skills in catering, tourism and construction pick up work far away from home each summer and this helps them through the leaner winter months.

Open and closed questions

Good interviewers know about open and closed questions and they use them deliberately to obtain the information they need.

Open questions are used to encourage you to talk about yourself, your background and experience, and your feelings about the job you are applying for. The words of the question are purposely chosen to ensure that you cannot easily give a simple one-word answer. Open questions often begin with phrases such as: 'How do you feel about . . .?' or 'What do you think are the most . . .?'

If you've done your homework, these questions won't surprise you so you should be able to answer in a relaxed yet informed manner. Make sure that you are answering the question rather than simply repeating a rehearsed speech, and keep a close check on your interviewer's body language. Is he nodding and encouraging you to continue? Have you engaged his attention or is he distractedly waiting for you to finish so that he can ask the next question?

Closed questions are used to obtain hard information. They usually require short answers. A closed question often begins with 'Do you . . .?', and the usual response has to be 'Yes I do' or 'No I don't'. An interviewer will use closed questions either to check basic factual information or press you into making a firm statement if he feels that your responses to his open questions are too vague or woolly. When you are faced with questions such as these you have to come off the fence and answer appropriately. A firm answer to a closed question is always preferable to an indecisive or imprecise one which could imply that you are being less than honest in your response.

Open learning see *Distance learning*

Organisational ability

Most jobs require a degree of organisational ability. In some jobs you may have to lead a team of staff and make sure that they are in the right place at the right time to be effective. In other jobs, you may have to ensure that schedules are met and that materials arrive in the right place on time. Sometimes you may have to organise your own work and decide which tasks take priority over others.

How can you show an employer that you have the required organisational ability? Perhaps you have enough evidence from your previous job but, if this is your first attempt at a 'management' post, you may have to use illustrations of your ability from elsewhere. Are you a member of any clubs or societies? Have you ever had to organise an event or take part in fund-raising? What about your family life? Have you brought up children and had to manage on a small income? If you have, you must have some organisational ability. Don't sell yourself short; you are probably a better organiser than you think.

Further information
Get Organised, Odette Pollar (Kogan Page, 1993)

P

Part-time work

Whatever kind of job you are hoping to get, full-time or part-time, the same general principles apply. If you are hoping to find part-time work, you will still need to look out for advertisements, prepare letters of application and attend interviews. You have a slight advantage over someone looking for a full-time job, though, because more and more jobs are being offered on a part-time basis.

As far as an employer is concerned, there are several advantages in having a portion of the workforce employed in this way. If trade picks up, there is a pool of skilled labour able to help out by working a few extra hours during peak periods. It also means that there is a better chance of covering the work of staff who are absent because of illness or annual leave. Part-time staff who work extra hours are often paid at their hourly rate whereas full-time staff would demand time and a half payment for overtime.

None of this should put you off applying for a part-time job. The arrangement you make with the boss may be ideal for both of you provided that, from the outset, you both clearly understand the hours of work and the days on which you are supposed to attend. You may need to explain the extent to which you can be flexible and your working limits. If your employer knows that you have to collect your child from school at a half past three every afternoon, you won't be put in the embarrassing position of having to refuse to work beyond that time. For your part, you must accept that your employer needs you at work on the days and times you have agreed. When you are at work, you must give the same commitment and energy per hour as any full-time employee. Your hours of work may be part-time but your commitment to the job must be unquestionable.

When looking for part-time work, you often have to spread your net wide. Some employers don't bother to advertise. They rely on existing staff to suggest suitable candidates or they keep a file of letters from people who have written in asking about part-time opportunities. They are often able to recruit part-time staff from among their own workforce. Women, for example, sometimes prefer to take a part-time option for a few years while they bring up a family. If you are looking for part-time work tell your friends to let you know if they hear of any. Check newsagents' noticeboards, and the smaller classified ads in the local press. You might even think of putting in an advertisement yourself.

Finally, you could team up with another jobhunter seeking part-time work and apply for full-time jobs on a job-share basis, which is becoming more common nowadays. It could be an intriguing possibility for an employer.

Pensions

The pension arrangements which a company makes for its employees are important aspects of every job's remuneration package. Some companies offer attractive pension opportunities and others offer none at all. When you are in your twenties retirement may seem like a distant horizon and thoughts of a retirement pension are probably not on your agenda. As you get older, however, pension arrangements become increasingly important, especially when you are looking for or changing a job.

Company pension packages are not compulsory. You don't have to become a member of any scheme which you don't understand or don't like. You are free to shop around until you find your preferred package.

Pension arrangements can be complicated, especially if you are hoping to transfer your contributions from one scheme to another.

Further information
Free, up-to-date information about State retirement pensions is available in a brochure *NP 46 A Guide to Retirement Pensions* obtainable from the Department of Social Security, Richmond House, 79 Whitehall, London SW1A 2NS; 0171-210 3000.

Information, advice and explanations of other pension packages can be obtained from independent financial advisers. Membership of the professional association of independent financial advisers (FIMBRA) ensures that advice is fair and independent. Yellow Pages offers local names and addresses of FIMBRA members. Alternatively, you can phone FIMBRA on 0171–538 8860 to obtain information about advisers currently approved by the Association in your area.

Advisers who are not members of FIMBRA may be associated with a single insurance company and they are often only able to offer advice regarding that company's services.

Permanent employment

Whether we like it or not the idea of permanent employment, as it was understood by our fathers and grandfathers, is gone for good. Whatever job you hope to get, it probably won't see you through your working life. The chances are that you'll change your company as well as your job but, even if you remain with the same firm, your work will be transformed during the course of the next 10 or 15 years. For many of us 'permanent employment' will be achieved only through our ability to move between jobs with the minimum of anxiety or unemployment.

Permanent jobs are becoming harder to find and short-term contracts are on the increase. They allow an organisation to make rapid adjustments to the size, shape and scale of operation in response to the changing business environment. Think carefully if you are offered a short-term contract; don't dismiss it immediately. Short-term work can look good on a CV if it is with a prestigious company, and in a dynamic successful organisation it could be a safer bet than a so-called permanent job in a company which has its back to the wall. In a world where change is the only permanent feature, getting a job has to be a little like playing chess; you need to think one or two moves ahead. What extra skills and experience will this job give me? What new doors will it open up? Does this job move me further towards my goals? If you are unemployed, a short-term contract of even just two months is worth considering.

Person specification

Once a vacancy has been agreed, many employers write a person specification as well as a **job description**. A person specification is an attempt to identify the ideal candidate for the job. An employer tries to describe the background the person should have, the type and level of qualifications he or she would need to do the job well, the level of fitness required, the previous experience needed to fulfil the tasks, and the temperament which the job requires. He may also think about the location of the job and make a statement about whether it would be unsuitable for people with particular types of **disability**.

A person specification can be used in a number of ways. Initially, it is a tool for producing a shortlist of candidates from a large number of applications. The person specification, for example, may require the successful candidate to hold a clean driving licence. Automatically, therefore, the company can discount any applicant who doesn't appear to meet this requirement. It may require proven ability in maths or experience of handling people in difficult situations. Once again, when there is no evidence of either of these, the employer can reject more applications until he arrives at a small group who appear to fit the bill. If the shortlist is still too long, he may now decide to take up references on these candidates to see if that helps him to reduce the list even further. Finally, he will have a small group of applicants whom he wishes to interview.

Equal opportunity employers often take the process a stage further and use the person specification at interview to explain how they arrived at the decision to employ this particular candidate in favour of the four or five other interviewees. The interview will be used as a means of testing each candidate to see if all the requirements of the person specification are met. They may know, for example, that you have a driving licence, but it wasn't clear from your application whether it was clean or not. Testing candidates against the requirements of a well-written person specification allows an employer to prove that the decision not to employ someone was based on a requirement of the job rather than a view about suitability based on ethnic background, religion or disability.

Testing applications against the requirements of a person specification is a good method of reducing a large number to a manageable shortlist. If you don't take the time to make a good detailed application, an employer may assume that you don't meet the requirements.

In many instances, employers who use person specifications discover that, in theory at least, they have a shortlist of people, all of whom could do the job well. When it comes to the interview, the successful candidate is the one with the most appropriate temperament and personality.

Photocopies

Photocopiers are your friends. Never send a **letter of application**, an **application form** or a **curriculum vitae** without taking a photocopy first. If you have taken the time to list all your previous employers and work out the starting and finishing dates for each job, if you have spent a couple of hours explaining in a letter why you want to be a nursery nurse or an engineer, and if you have carefully listed all the schools you attended and the examinations you took, it would be crazy to put all that information in the post without keeping a copy. You may not need the information again for five or six years, but most application forms ask for the same information and, anyway, it's always easier to update an old document than start again from scratch.

Also, before you fill in an application form, remember to take a photocopy first and use that as a draft.

You can take photocopies in most high-street printshops. Alternatively, most public libraries have photocopying facilities.

Playing to your strengths

When you look at a **job description**, try to read between the lines and work out the type of person being sought. If you were a manager looking for the ideal candidate for this job, what would you be hoping to find in your ideal candidate? Make a list of the qualities you think are necessary to do the job well.

Now, take a look at yourself and make a list of the skills, experience and qualities which you feel you have. How do the two lists compare? First, look at your strong points. These are what you need to emphasise in your **letter of application** and at **interview**. Think of the questions you may be asked and the sorts of answer you can give to underline your strengths.

Now let's take a look at your weaknesses. Are you short on experience? Well, two years' good experience in an up-to-date organisation can be worth much more than five or ten years' experience in a company which destroyed your motivation by refusing to recognise your potential and insisting on using out-moded methods. Quality of experience is more important than length of service. What about skills? OK, you may have been out of work for a while and you may need to brush up your technical knowledge or skills. So tell an employer of your enthusiasm and willingness to learn or retrain. Do you think your age may worry an employer? It shouldn't but remember that age is always on your side if you take a positive view about it.

So what's left to worry about? Probably only your temperament. This is something which you cannot change, and if you are worried that you may not have the patience to do a certain type of work, or if you feel that you may be better suited working elsewhere, perhaps you should ask yourself whether this job is for you. Should you direct your energies to something which suits you better?

Positive attitude

Positive thinking and a belief in your abilities can be a major factor in successful jobhunting. Look at the **job description**. How many of those responsibilities are daunting? Is there anything there that you couldn't tackle? List those aspects of the job of which you already have experience – and don't restrict yourself to thinking merely about previous work experience. There is a life outside work, and your experience there can be just as valuable to an employer.

Think also about your own character and make up. Do the requirements of this job suit you? Some jobs require patience, others require an ability to work under pressure and cope with stress; some jobs demand a self-motivated person who can work without supervision, and others need people who can cope with highly detailed repetitive work. Do the requirements of this job match up to the sort of person you are? If so, do you have any examples? Finally, ask yourself honestly if you really want this job. This can be more important to an employer than technical skill. You can train someone to do a job, but you cannot easily make them want to do it. Poor attitudes which have developed over years can be hard to change.

Careers officers in one region recently telephoned a cross-section of employers who had fired young employees during the previous 12 months. They asked why the young people had lost their jobs. In almost every case, employers said it was because of 'attitude' problems. Lack of technical skill didn't come into the picture.

One major national employer sums it up: 'Give me the "right" person and we'll train them to do the job.' If an employer wants you he will be prepared to invest in you and give you the training you require to become effective.

Further information
How to Develop a Positive Attitude, Elwood N Chapman (Kogan Page, 1988)

Stay Positive! It's All a Matter of Attitude, Elwood N Chapman (Kogan Page, 1993)

Preparation

You may be the best person for the job. Your skills and qualifications may be unbeatable, and your experience may be just what the employer needs, but without sound preparation and attention to the smaller details you could still be unsuccessful. Getting a job requires a disciplined, methodical approach from the moment you begin the process.

Preparation begins even before you make that first phone call asking for an application form and further details of the vacancy. Rehearse what you are going to say and make sure that you have a pencil and paper with you.

Read through any **job description** or further information sent to you and prepare answers to as many questions as you can think of. If you are asked to give the names and addresses of referees, telephone them and let them know that they may be asked to write a reference about you; they need time to prepare too.

Have a good **curriculum vitae** ready; you may need to produce it at speed and, even if you have ten days to complete and return your application, don't leave it to the last minute. Allocate time now to getting it written.

Prepare your interview clothes and hang them in the wardrobe ready for use. You may need them at short notice. If any need drycleaning or pressing, do it now. Get your shoes polished and make an appointment with the hairdresser. The more you can do now, the less you have to worry about on the day of the interview.

Set aside some time for research to get the information you need about the job and the company and, if you need to make childminding arrangements, explore the possibilities now. If you are invited to attend an interview, think about how you are going to get there. How long will it take? Where can you park? Should you use public transport? What if it's raining?

With so many questions and so much to do, you can't possibly work through the entire process without writing lists. **Checklists** are the secret to success. Write down what you need to do, and tick the items off as you do them. Just think, as you make your preparations, you may be the only one taking this much trouble – now that's a hopeful thought, isn't it?

Professionalism

There is an old saying: 'A professional is someone who can do the job whether he feels like it or not.' Professionalism is about doing everything to the best of your ability. When you apply it to getting a job it means that you take time and care over your application, you prepare for your interview as well as you can, and you take pride in your efforts. It also means that you don't give up if you don't get the job you wanted at the first attempt. A professional has staying power and persistence. He can roll with the punches, pick himself up, and get on with his life and his jobhunting.

When you apply for a job, no one owes you anything but you owe it to yourself to give it your best shot – even if the job is only temporary and part-time.

Prospects

You can be trained to do some jobs in a matter of a few hours. Within a week you can be up to speed and earning the full rate for the job. In a few years' time, if the job still exists, you will probably be earning roughly the same wage. You'll be no more highly skilled than before and it will be easy for an employer to replace you. After all, it will only take an hour or so to train a new recruit. In this job you have no prospects.

By contrast, some jobs require specialist skill and knowledge. It takes time to develop the expertise required so your wages may be low until you have mastered all the techniques. When you are fully trained, however, you will be a recognised skilled worker and your wages will rise to reflect the special knowledge and skill acquired. An employer who has invested time and effort in you will be reluctant to lose you. When you are looking for permanent work try to take a long view. Such jobs may pay poorly to begin with but, five years from now, you may be pleased that you opted for a job with prospects.

Punctuality

It is important to be on time for each and every appointment with an employer. Ideally, you should arrive at the office or factory ten minutes early. You can use this time to collect your thoughts and check your tie/your hair before you are invited into his office. That way, you enter in a calm and collected fashion.

If you are unfamiliar with the company's location, or if you are unsure about public transport or parking facilities, always try to do a dry run and visit the company a few days before your interview at the same time of day as your appointment. Don't go in; just stop at the door and check how long it took you. That way you'll know how long to allow for getting there on the day.

It is always better to be a half hour early for an appointment than even one minute late. If you arrive far too early, take a walk around the block. You can pick up a lot of useful information about a company from the neighbourhood in which it is located, especially if it serves the local community. A walk around can tell you a lot about the customers it is trying to serve.

Once you have a job, start punctually each day, and allow for traffic jams and delays in public transport by leaving home early.

Qualifications

In England and Wales GCEs used to be the accepted school-leaver's qualification. Then came CSE and now we have GCSE. A grade 1 CSE was considered to be the equivalent of a pass at GCE level. Today a grade C GCSE has the same currency. A levels have long been the accepted standard by which 18-year-old school-leavers are judged. In Scotland standard grade SCEs equate to GCSEs and higher grade SCEs are the Scottish equivalent of A levels.

The introduction of vocationally oriented level 2 GNVQs is an attempt to give equal status to 'vocational' qualifications. A GNVQ at this level is equivalent to four GCSEs. Level 3 GNVQs are worth the same as two A levels.

In further and higher education there is a confusing range of available qualifications. The chart opposite summarises the better known qualifications, indicating their relationship to NVQ levels 1 to 5.

Qualities

You can easily measure an electrician's ability. You can test his competence to re-wire a house or install a range of new kitchen appliances. You can check his work for neatness, accuracy and economy. You can test the speed of his work to ensure that his tasks are completed on time and that he can keep to a schedule, and you can run a check on his work to ensure that the installation meets current safety requirements.

It is more difficult to measure a person's cheerfulness when dealing with members of the public, or the ability to inspire confidence among customers and staff. How do you measure loyalty, enthusiasm, honesty, leadership, vision, resilience and tolerance? Every job requires a level of skill, but every job also needs a certain mix of qualities and, despite the difficulties in measuring them, employers often place as much value on qualities as skill. You can get an A level in history, a BTEC in business and finance, or a City and Guilds in electrical installation, but there is

Employment

Starting age			NVQ level
21+	POSTGRADUATE		**5**
18+	DEGREE 3 or 4 years Entry – 2 or 3 A levels or BTEC National or GNVQ level 3 or technical and day release		**4**
18+	HIGHER NATIONAL DIPLOMA 2/3 years – vocational subjects only Entry – 1 or more A levels or BTEC National or GNVQ level 3 or technical and day release		
17+ / 16+	BTEC NATIONAL C&G advanced craft courses GNVQ level 3 2 years Entry – 4 GCSEs at grade C or good GNVQ level 2 or BTEC First Diploma	A LEVELS 2 or 3 years Entry – 4/5 GCSEs at C or above preferably with an A or B in the subjects you wish to study	**3**
16+	BTEC FIRST DIPLOMA C&G craft courses GNVQ level 2 craft 1 year only Entry – GCSE in maths and English	GCSE 4 good passes grade C or above Youth Training to NVQ level 2	**2**
16+	GNVQ foundation level	Craft foundation subjects. GCSE passes – Grade D	Youth Training	**1**
Starting age	Year 11		NVQ level

no examination yet which offers a qualification in leadership, integrity or energy.

When you are invited to an interview, an employer may have already convinced himself that you have the necessary skills to do the job. He may have seen your qualifications and certificates, and he may know from a previous employer that you are competent at your job. At times such as these, qualities will be the central issue.

Think about what qualities an employer would like to see in someone applying for a job such as this and then look carefully at yourself. What examples can you think of which will indicate that you have the qualities he requires? Don't restrict yourself to examples from previous jobs; think about other aspects of your life. Members of sports teams can show their willingness to work alongside others to achieve a common goal. Voluntary charity workers can illustrate their concern and commitment to causes in which they believe. They can also use the same example to show that they are trustworthy and conscientious workers. School-leavers who were prefects or organisers of school societies can use these examples to demonstrate leadership quality, drive and organisational ability.

Questionnaires

Some employers are losing faith in references. It is rare for a candidate to offer the name of a referee who is going to be unsupportive of his application, so making sense of references can become an exercise in reading between the lines. They are also criticised for being imprecise. To combat this, some employers ask referees to complete questionnaires which ask for precise information about the topics that interest them. Referees are asked to tick appropriate boxes from 'very good' through 'average' to 'very poor'.

Recruitment agencies

Recruitment agencies will find staff for a fee which is charged to the employer, *not* the jobseeker. Companies can use the expertise of professional interviewers rather than working through the process themselves. Good recruitment agencies get to know their client companies well. They try to ensure that they know the atmosphere, the benefits, the number of employees and the training policy of each company. They know the qualities each company is looking for in its staff and the level of speed, accuracy and skill required. They take time and trouble to find suitable people to fill vacancies as they arise. Their credibility is based on their ability to provide suitable recruits who can fill vacancies with a minimum of fuss and disruption.

When you see an advertisement for a job placed by a recruitment agency you will often be given far more information than you would normally expect. In most instances you will be interviewed for the job by the recruitment agency on behalf of the client company. The interviewers are usually highly experienced and professional so you can expect to undergo a fairly thorough interview. Afterwards, whether you get the job or not, you may be offered the chance of feedback on how you performed. This, in itself, can be a helpful means of improving your future technique. A recruitment agency may be willing to keep your name on file and approach you if a similar vacancy crops up. Most agencies are discreet. They understand that you may not want your present employer to know that you are considering moving on. They often work outside normal office hours so you can talk confidentially to their staff.

References

Most application forms ask you for the names and addresses of two or three people who can be approached by the company for information about you. When you are preparing your **curriculum vitae** you should include such names.

It is almost certain that an employer who is seriously considering inviting you to an interview will contact these people. Usually, employers like to have information about your performance in the workplace. They like to get a view of you from someone you have worked for. Ideally, they would like a reference from your present boss. In the public service, you would be hard-pressed to avoid this. In the private sector, however, it is recognised that not all candidates wish their present employer to know that they are considering leaving his employment. On that basis it is reasonable to offer names of alternative referees stating why you do not wish your current employer to be approached without prior consultation with yourself.

If you cannot provide the names and addresses of two people who can report on your ability and character in the workplace, your second referee could be someone who can offer complementary evidence of your suitability for this job – for example, someone of good standing in the community who can enthuse about your personal qualities, your honesty and integrity. References from within and without the workplace can be a powerful combination which enables an interviewer to get a picture of the whole person.

If you are just leaving college, your tutor should know you well enough to write with some authority about your academic achievements and your contribution to the social life of the institution, so a good second referee might be a supervisor from your work-experience placement or your boss from the company where you worked during the last vacation.

Whoever you choose, make sure that you have their permission to offer their names as referees and brief them well about the job you are applying for. A general reference stating 'This person will be an asset to any company fortunate enough to employ her . . . ' is all right, but a reference which is written with a specific job in mind can be much more powerful – 'Her voluntary work with young children allied to her commercial experience give me no hesitation in recommending this person to you for the post of school secretary at . . . '.

Take some time to talk through the job with your referees. They're going to be working on your behalf so let them know what the job is all about and why it is important to you.

Research

There is no substitute for good research. It is an essential part of your preparation. It gives you the background knowledge which you need to make a strong application for a job. When you apply you need to know as much as you can about the company. At least you should know what it makes, or the service it offers. Make an effort to discover what its customers are like and why this particular company is different from others which seem to offer similar goods or services. Try to find out about the size of its operation and check out its advertisements. How does this company make its sales pitch? Are its goods or services cheaper, faster or better quality than those of its competitors? Take a walk around the area to discover what the clients are like and, finally, make a visit to the local library to see whether the company has been in the news during the past few years.

Routine

Routine, the very thing which you may have hated about your previous job, can be a life-saver during periods of unemployment. Getting a job demands discipline. You have to make a full-time job out of it so get into a regular routine of checking newspapers for advertisements, writing letters, visiting the **Jobcentre** and phoning around employers. Set yourself some targets and deadlines. What can you achieve by the end of the week? How long will it take you to contact every likely employer listed in Yellow Pages? How many should you contact each day? Enrol on some courses (many are offered at reduced rates to unemployed people) to improve your skills and plan some free time into your schedule so that you can still meet friends and maintain contact with the rest of the world. Getting a job takes energy and it can be time-consuming but if you are unemployed you have plenty of that to spare. Use it constructively.

S

School's out!

Each year from June onwards the numbers of jobhunters swell as thousands of young people leave school and college to test their luck and skill in the market-place. Whatever educational course you are studying you are probably busy during your final year, but don't leave your jobhunting to the last minute or you'll find yourself competing with many more people than you need to. Begin your search for employment by writing to companies in the January of your final academic year. Let the world know that you are eager to find employment and tell everyone when you will be available to start. Remember the old saying about the early bird.

Scottish Certificate of Education

These school examinations are taken in a variety of subjects in Scotland. There are two grades of SCE. Standard, previously ordinary grade SCEs, are usually taken at 15 or 16 years of age and students are awarded certificates graded from 1 to 7. Passes at grades 1, 2 or 3 are considered to be equivalent to GCSE passes. Higher grade SCEs, sometimes referred to as revised higher grade SCEs, are usually taken in a range of subjects at 16 or 17 years of age. Successful students are awarded passes at A, B or C grades. A pass at A or B grade is regarded as the equivalent of an A level GCE pass. Two grade C passes are regarded as equivalent to one A level GCE pass.

Scottish Vocational Education Council

SCOTVEC is responsible for the design and accreditation of a wide range of job-related courses and modules of further education in Scotland. Levels of study range from non-advanced courses through to Higher National Certificate (HNC), Higher National Diploma (HND) and professional development awards. The qualifications are frequently structured around modules and units similar to NVQ qualifications which are available in England and Wales. The Council also produces a Record of Education and Training (RET) on which all SCOTVEC awards are recorded for each candidate. There is a highly developed range of distance learning packages in SCOTVEC subjects.

Further information
Details of SCOTVEC awards and the range of courses available may be obtained from the Scottish Vocational Education Council, Hanover House, 24 Douglas Street, Glasgow G2 7NQ; 0141 248 7900

Selection tests

Many organisations use selection tests in their recruitment process. Sometimes they want to measure your technical skill and aptitude for the job. Electricity companies, for example, usually test would-be apprentices for their mathematical skill and understanding of the general principles of electricity. They also test for colour blindness. Confusing red and green cables could have catastrophic results! They aren't looking for experts but they need to know that you have a good basic understanding of the subjects and an ability to learn more. Police forces and prison services put their candidates through a series of examinations which test physical well-being as well as general knowledge. The armed forces have a wide range of tests which they apply to candidates depending on which branch of activity they are aiming for. At officer level, practical tests and challenges are used to determine leadership qualities. Some factories require candidates to complete tests to indicate how well developed their hand and eye co-ordination is. Many companies give prospective secretaries a keyboard and simple bookkeeping test. Careers officers are usually able to advise on which companies expect candidates to undergo a selection test.

When you are invited to attend an **interview**, you are usually asked to phone the company to confirm that you will attend. If you feel that you may be asked to take a test, it will do you no harm to ask when you phone to thank them for the invitation to the interview.

Written tests are usually time-limited. You get a number of questions to answer in a relatively short time. Success depends on your ability to answer the questions quickly and accurately. Don't worry about not answering all the questions in the time given. Many of the tests are designed to ensure that it would be extremely unlikely for anyone to achieve this. When you are doing such a test, keep up your pace by skipping over any questions which are too difficult, concentrate on answering those which you find easy and then come back to the harder ones if there is any time left at the end. When you are asked to take a test, apply the same rules as if you were going for an interview. Dress appropriately, arrive early, try to stay calm and be pleasant to whoever you meet.

Further information
How to Pass Selection Tests, Mike Bryon and Sanjay Modha (Kogan Page, 1991)

Self-employment

In your attempts to get a job, don't dismiss the idea of becoming self-employed. It can be an attractive possibility but you need to think it through carefully first. You will need to be highly motivated and, in the early days at least, you must be prepared to work long hours for little reward. You will also need to have a marketable skill or service. People who are successful in self-employment are risk-takers but their risks are carefully calculated. Frequently they have to make substantial investments of their own money in the venture and they usually have to convince bank managers and other financiers of the strength of their ideas.

Before taking such a step, ask yourself if you are fit and energetic enough for self-employment. How would you feel about taking business calls at 9 pm on a Friday evening or spending an entire Sunday putting together a tender for a job which you may not be offered? Try to take a realistic look at the business you are thinking about establishing. Do you have the skills to produce these goods or offer these services and, if so, what are your chances of success? Is your idea unique or are there other people swimming in the same pond?

You will also need to consider how to finance your business and see it through the early years when the outgoings may often seem to be larger than your income. Most likely, if you seek a business loan you will have to produce a business plan which offers a realistic estimate of the initial costs you will incur and the income your activities will generate. The plan will have to highlight periods when outgoings could exceed income and predict eventual profits. The plan may need to be detailed and explain how you arrive at the unit cost of the item you intend to make or sell. Initially, many small businesses make over-optimistic predictions about how cheaply they can market their goods or services. Only later do they appreciate the full extent of the expenditure which they incur through their activities. Poor preparation or an over-optimistic view of the possibilities is a major cause of cash-flow problems for many fledgling businesses. As in all things – careful research and preparation are the key to success.

By now, it should be clear that skill in one particular aspect of work is not enough to guarantee successful self-employment. Electrical skills, for example, are the basic requirement for a self-employed electrician but, in themselves, they will not guarantee success. To manage his own business well, an electrician needs to be able to work out the price of jobs and to advertise and market his services and manage his time effectively. He should be highly organised, able to understand simple bookkeeping and office practice, and be a good decision-maker, supervisor and negotiator.

If you are excited by the challenges of self-employment there is a good deal of help and advice available. Most banks offer special support for new businesses which includes free advice on business planning and initial financial support packages. Your local **Training and Enterprise Council** (TEC; LEC in Scotland) is responsible for business and enterprise training. TECs can help you with raising finance, market research, taxation, viability, legal matters, business plans and cash-flow forecasts. You may also be able to discuss the possibility of obtaining a business start-up allowance during the crucial first year of operation.

Further information

The Small Business Action Kit, 4th edition, John Rosthorn, Andrew Haldane, Edward Blackwell and John Wholey (Kogan Page, 1994)

The Daily Telegraph Guide to Self-Employment, *Working for Yourself*, 15th edition, Godfrey Golzen (Kogan Page, 1994). It is a goldmine of information for anyone considering taking the plunge. A list of helpful start-up books is available from Kogan Page.

Self-respect

You are a human being with dignity and self-respect. You have beliefs and values central to your make-up and you know that some people hold you dear. Getting a job is important but it is not the only purpose of your existence. Pity the poor employer who cannot see your true worth. An employer who fails to appreciate your potential or who undervalues your experience takes nothing from you. You remain as skilled and experienced as before. It is his loss not yours. There may be times when you need to work at a level beneath your capability or lower your sights and take on work which carries less responsibility than before but you are no less a person for that.

Seeking a job can be a hard, lonely and depressing experience. Failure to secure a couple of jobs can damage your self-image. In work or out of it, you can keep your self-respect by putting more energy into those other aspects of your life which are important to you and giving more to those for whom you care. If you are active in promoting the well-being of others you will be valued and the respect you earn will ensure that you remain aware of your worth.

Shortlisting

Shortlisting is the process which employers go through to reduce a large number of applicants to a small number of people they would like to know better. It can be a difficult job and the initial screening processes can be brutal. Some employers, for example, refuse to consider applications which are untidy or carelessly prepared. Don't, for example, expect to get an interview if you spell the manager's name wrongly or if you change the colour of ink halfway through your letter. If your **job application** isn't neat, what are you telling the employer about your interest in the job he has to offer?

Some employers arrive at their shortlist by comparing each application against their ideal. They discount any which don't appear to meet their requirements. This method can often reduce 30 or 40 applications to a more manageable pile of five or six who may be worth interviewing. Employers usually take up references on these and may use the information they receive to discount one or two more.

It is important to understand two things about the shortlisting process. First, you can be sure that if you are shortlisted your application is being treated seriously and you are a real contender for the job. Second, and perhaps more important, if you aren't shortlisted it is probably because you didn't give the employer enough information. If this job is perfect for you, let the employer know. He's not a mind reader and the application form alone will not be enough to tell him how good you are. Put a letter in with your application and let your skill and enthusiasm shine through – don't sell yourself short.

Small businesses

Small companies stay in business by being highly flexible and capable of adapting to rapidly changing situations. Staff in many small companies are expected to be multi-skilled. These companies cannot afford to employ specialists. In effect, the more skills you can offer the better your chances. If you can turn your hand to a variety of tasks you may have the edge over more highly qualified candidates. If a small company loses a member of staff, the loss can represent a significant portion of the workforce. In a small company the person who left may have been the only one on the payroll with those particular skills. Even if no one leaves, one unexpected contract can be large enough to send a small company scurrying to the **Jobcentre** urgently seeking additional staff. The important message is that often, when a small company needs a new member of staff, it needs him yesterday!

When you are looking for a job, stay in contact with the small operations. Ask your friends to let you know if they hear of anyone leaving, or of any company getting a large contract. Write to all the small businesses in your area who employ people with your range of skills, let them know that you are available at short notice and give them an easy means of contacting you. Follow up your letter with a phone call a couple of weeks later – just to check that your letter was received.

Small companies are usually free of the procedures which govern larger operations. When you apply for a job in a small company you may be expected to write a letter and provide a CV but small companies often don't have application forms. A direct approach to a small business can be very productive. A telephone call can result in an invitation to visit the following day. Knock on the door at the right time and you may be invited to roll your sleeves up and get started straightaway.

If you are invited to an **interview** in an organisation such as this, you can expect to be interviewed by one person rather than a panel and your interviewer may also be the owner of the company. He will probably know everything about his business and his customers and, if he is successful, he will be highly motivated and hard working. He'll be looking for the same qualities in you but he may not be a highly skilled interviewer. His questions may be poorly phrased and there may be some uncomfortable pauses while he thinks of the next question. You may need to help him along a little.

Smile

It is a scientifically proved fact that you use fewer muscles in a smile than a frown. A cheerful smile will lead your potential employer to think that you are confident and relaxed – even if in reality you are a quivering jelly. A warm smile and the offer of a handshake when you enter the room can break the ice and give a good first impression. More important, though, smiles are infectious. Your smile will provoke smiles in others. It's a good way to start any meeting and – if this meeting happens to be an interview – all the better!

Speculative enquiries

Don't wait for the right job to be advertised. Make a list of all those companies who employ people with your type of skills and let them know that you are looking for a job. Many employers are popular and have no need to spend money on advertising vacancies when they know of several people who are waiting for the chance of an **interview**. A speculative letter should be short and to the point. State your interest in working within that organisation, tell the employer what kind of job you are seeking, what skills you have, and how you can be easily contacted. An enclosed CV will supply enough information about qualifications and previous experience.

Ask whether you could make an appointment to visit the company to discuss the possibility of employment there. Address the letter to the owner, manager or personnel officer by name. If you are not sure of the name, telephone and ask who the most appropriate person would be. Make sure to include a stamped self-addressed envelope (SAE) and then see what happens.

You have to accept that some companies will not reply. Others will not wish to see you but will keep your details on file until a suitable vacancy arises. Some, however, may invite you for an informal interview, a discussion or a chat. At such times, make all the preparations that you would for a formal interview. Check your dress, be punctual and be prepared. This visit may be informal, there may be no job at present but you will want to make a good impression and they wouldn't invite you to visit them unless they had some interest in you.

After the visit build on the relationship that you have established by sending a further letter to the person you met, thanking him for taking the time to see you, and emphasising your continued enthusiasm for a job within the organisation. The whole exercise may have cost you no more than the price of three first class postage stamps, but you may have moved a long way down the road towards getting a job.

A good general speculative letter can be sent, with a few changes, to a wide range of companies, but don't send out photocopies or you'll give the impression that your letter is little more than a mailshot. Rewriting each letter can be time-consuming but if you have access to a word processor you should be able to contact a fairly wide range of companies without too much trouble. If you are unemployed, stamps can be an expensive item, but some **jobclubs** offer free stamps. Otherwise, keep costs down by being more precise about which companies to include on your list of targets. Give companies scores out of ten depending on your assessment of whether they employ people with your range of skills and write only to companies which score high on your list.

Student loans

If you are under 50 years old, and thinking about improving your educational qualifications through a full-time course of higher education, you may be eligible for a government loan. Loans were introduced in 1990 to help students meet their living costs. If you are studying a course for which a **grant** could be available, you are also entitled to apply for a student loan. You may borrow up to a set amount each year.

You will not be asked to start paying back the loan until the April after you finish or leave your course but you can start to pay it back earlier if you wish. The amount you owe will be linked to inflation so that the 'value' of the amount you pay back will be broadly the same as the 'value' of the amount you borrowed. See also **Career development loans**.

Further information

The Department for Education, Publications Centre, PO Box 2193, London E15 2EU; 0171-925 5000

The Scottish Office Education Department, New St Andrews House, St James Centre, Edinburgh EH1 3SY; 0131-556 8400

Support groups

When you are trying to get a job there are a number of good reasons for getting together with other people in the same situation. Support groups can offer practical help and encouragement. You should be able to obtain information about local **jobclubs** from the **Jobcentre**. Some jobclubs have telephones, computers and word processors available for use. Here, you can put together a standard **curriculum vitae**, **letters of application**, and **speculative enquiry** letters. Many jobclubs also organise mock interviews and offer training in **interview technique**. They also maintain libraries and lists of employers' names and addresses. Best of all, meeting other jobhunters enables you to dispel the damaging sense of isolation that unemployment encourages.

Local colleges frequently play host to self-help groups of unemployed people and organisers are also able to offer reduced price admission to a range of courses which can increase or update your

SUPPORT GROUPS

skills. If you need support in basic skills, the local college should be able to help here too. Some professional institutes may offer services to unemployed members.

Further information

If you are considering **self-employment** there are a number of organisations which offer support. The **Training and Enterprise Council** (TEC, or LEC in Scotland) or your local Chamber of Commerce should be able to put you in touch with them.

Details of all local jobclubs, local colleges and voluntary groups in your area are available in public libraries.

T

Telephones

Even if you are naturally easy and relaxed on the telephone, there is much to be said for spending a few minutes preparing what you intend to say when you call someone to enquire about a job. If you have a good telephone manner you will create a good first impression. Rehearse what you are going to say and write down the questions you intend to ask. You may be asked for your address and telephone number, so if you are staying with friends make sure that you have a note of these handy.

Before you call, choose a phone in a quiet location where you will not be disturbed. If you are at home, ban everyone else from the room before you begin and make sure that the radio and TV are turned off. If you are using a public phone make sure that you have plenty of units left on your phonecard or, if it has a coinbox, that you have a good supply of suitable coins. When you speak, try to smile. The person at the other end of the line cannot see you, of course, but you'd be surprised how your smile can affect your tone of voice, making you sound pleasant and relaxed.

Finally, be prepared for an answerphone. Many people don't like leaving messages, but if you come up against one, don't hang up; leave your message speaking slowly and clearly. At such times you'll be glad that you prepared and wrote down what you intended to say.

Teleworking

The technology is now mostly available to enable large numbers of company employees to work from home. They'll be giving up the concrete highway in favour of the 'technological superhighway'. Rather than move people it will soon be possible, and preferable, to move the information they need to do their jobs down fibre-optic cables into their own homes.

Already there is a growing band of people who work from home using personal computers, word processors, fax machines and modems.

Some teleworkers operate on a freelance basis, but others are fully employed by companies which allow them to spend a large portion of their time at home.

As the information superhighway develops, an increasing number of workers will have less need to visit the company office to do their jobs. A home-worker will be able to discuss problems with colleagues and bosses through TV-quality video connections, store and use huge amounts of video and digital data, and access computer information and applications as easily as if he were sitting at a desk today.

At present the lifestyle suits part-time workers and those with young children or other family commitments. They can schedule their work to take account of family need. If you're interested in the idea of teleworking on a freelance basis start by examining your skills in order to discover what sort of work you could undertake from home. Once your area of interest and expertise has been identified, take a long realistic look at the market potential for what you have to offer. Office skills lend themselves particularly well to this way of life – typing, data inputting, bookkeeping, accountancy, report writing, etc.

Unfortunately, teleworking has many attractions so it is hardly surprising that there are a lot of fish swimming in this particular sea. Do your market research well before investing in expensive computer equipment and software. If you are sure that there is a niche in the market for what you have to offer, begin building your client base by offering your services to a range of companies on a freelance basis. Make sure that your work is of the highest quality and always deliver on time. It may not produce enough work and income to meet all your needs but it gets you known and it allows employers to see the quality of your work. Who knows? It could lead to a full-time job – but maybe you'll find that the freelance teleworking life suits you better!

Temping

Some people enjoy moving from one company to another. They make a career out of temporary work which they pick up here and there. If you have the necessary skill and the right attitude, if you enjoy change and can adapt to different situations without effort, you can often pick up as much work as you need through temping. Sometimes you may be asked to take over a job to cover staff illness or maternity leave, on other occasions you may have to 'hold the fort' until a new permanent employee can be found. Sometimes you are brought in simply to help cope with an unexpected upturn in activity.

Many people think that temping applies only to office jobs but this is far from true. There are a large number of agencies which specialise in particular areas of work. There are, for example, agencies specialising in industrial work, catering, nursing, social work, and even physiotherapy. You may have to hunt down the names and addresses by looking through the small advertisements in professional journals in your public library. Some industrial temp agencies even provide transport to and from the work site.

Many recruitment agencies pride themselves on their ability to find an ideal temporary member of staff at short notice. A temp may receive a phone call from an agency in the morning and be expected to arrive at a company, cool, calm and ready for work after lunch. Agencies keep lists of suitable people and they look after them well. The best temps have special qualities and there is a constant demand for their services. Temping can be much harder than holding down a permanent job. Temps have to be versatile and are always under pressure to prove their worth. A new permanent member of staff may be given a week to adjust to a new job but a temp is expected to be effective within the first couple of hours in a new position, often using unfamiliar equipment. Temping requires a high level of professionalism. Recruitment agencies expect their temps to go that extra mile on behalf of the company where they have been placed. In effect, every temp is an ambassador for the recruitment agency which sent them.

Temping often suits young mothers who are available for work only during term time. University students on vacation are also popular with employers, particularly if they have keyboard skills. For young people it is an excellent way of discovering more about a range of working environments. A secretary, for example, may discover that she prefers a legal office to a bank. An office junior may find a small firm preferable to a large one.

This way of life often leads to the offer of permanent employment but many temps find that they prefer the constant change and excitement of temping.

Temporary work

If you are offered a temporary job – take it. When you are in work you are mixing with other workers, you hear what is happening around you in this company and in others. You are well placed to see how things are developing and where the opportunities lie. You are also moving at the right pace, using everyday working language, and keeping your skills up to date. For these reasons, people in work usually have less trouble in getting a new job than those who have been out of work for a while.

Use a temporary job as a stepping stone to get you closer to the permanent job you seek. Bear in mind also that things can change rapidly in business. Many companies offer temporary employment because it gives them a degree of flexibility. If the business doesn't grow as expected, their commitment to you is limited and they can adjust the size of their operation to the strength of the market. If things work out well, though, your temporary work could be extended or even made permanent.

In some areas of work, it is usual to take on a large number of temporary staff. Summer holiday camps and hotels, for example, depend on recruiting people for the summer season. Farms and orchards sometimes recruit workers to help with the harvest, and the Post Office takes on temporary staff to help with the extra volume of mail at Christmas. Temporary work abroad is a useful and practical way of improving language skills as well as earning money. The ability to speak a second language could help to improve your long-term job prospects.

Terms and conditions of employment

In law, you should be given a statement of the main terms and conditions of your employment. This is often written in a letter of appointment or given to you in the form of a contract. Many employers send it out within a few days of offering you the job but, if for any reason it is delayed, there are some good reasons why you shouldn't give notice to your present employer until you have seen and agreed the terms of your employment with your new employer. You may have been given a verbal offer of a job but this can be withdrawn. Play it safe; don't give up your present employment until you have something in writing from your new company.

If for any reason you have decided to start work without seeing or agreeing the written terms of employment, you should receive them within eight weeks of starting work. Ask for these written terms if you do not receive them.

Many letters or contracts contain a great deal of detail. In law, however, there is a basic minimum amount of information which you must be given:

- the name of the employer and employee;
- the title of the job;
- the commencement date;
- the rate of pay;
- the arrangements for making such payments (weekly or monthly, for example);
- details of your normal working hours;
- details of holiday arrangements (including bank holiday arrangements);

- arrangements for incapacity to work through sickness or injury (including sick pay and pension arrangements);
- disciplinary and grievance procedures;
- the length of notice required and, in the case of a short-term contract, the termination date.

Testimonials

People confuse testimonials with **references**. Testimonials are statements about you which people give to you to show other people. References are statements about you which are given in confidence to other people.

When you apply for a job, you are usually asked to supply the names and addresses of a couple of referees, people who can be approached to report on your character or work record. The strength of a reference is that it is unseen by you and, therefore, a referee is under no pressure from you to be anything but honest.

Employers view a testimonial as a weaker document because it has been written about you and given to you. After all, it is hardly likely that you would show a potential employer any statement about yourself which is not full of praise. Having said that, it is always worth including photocopies of good testimonials in your job applications. They may not carry the same weight as references but they are positive statements about you which can only do good.

Freelances find them particularly useful as 'advertising' material. When you have done a good piece of work, it is worth asking whether the manager of the company would be prepared to give you a testimonial. You can then show this to other companies as evidence of the quality of your service. If it does nothing else, it gives them an indication of other organisations you have worked for. If they want to check you out, they'll probably contact the writer of the testimonial and get a confidential view over the phone.

Time management

The ability to manage your time effectively is a crucial skill for jobhunters and there is much to be said for having a weekly planning session in which you note down the tasks you need to accomplish each day and the times when you need to do them. Some things will be daily occurrences such as checking the ads in the local paper. Other tasks may be less frequent. You may, for example, need to plan a regular trip to the library or jobclub, or lay time aside for completing a particular application form, or arranging to visit a company which has responded to one of your speculative letters. Perhaps you need to remind yourself about a couple of phone calls to be made and an appointment you have arranged with a childminder.

Each week you need to set targets for yourself. Send out another five or six speculative letters and follow up that lead about a job coming up in a company across town. You may have an interview to plan for, in which case a checklist of things to do between now and then will be a good way of keeping you on line.

Lay out your weekly plans on paper. Writing down your intentions helps to focus the mind and increases your chances of achieving your aims. Review the situation each week and note your success. Carry forward anything which you didn't achieve last week and add it to your plans for the coming week.

Training

Sometimes the gap between being unemployed and managing to get a job is narrow. People may fail to secure particular jobs because they lack a specific skill. Office workers, for example, may lose out because they are not familiar with a particular computer software package. Jobs in warehouses may be out of reach without a forklift truck driver's certificate. Often it is possible to identify exactly what skill you need in order to get a job. Training fills that gap and moves you closer to the type of work you seek. From time to time, government initiatives offer help to people who wish to undertake training in particular areas of work. Information can be obtained from **Jobcentres** and your local **Training and Enterprise Council**. These organisations also offer special training packages for people who have been unemployed for long periods.

Local colleges also offer a wide range of courses. Many are part-time evening classes and so it is possible to undertake training without hampering your jobseeking efforts.

If you know the area of work which interests you and are sure about the possibility of gaining employment after training, it might be worth exploring the opportunities that **career development loans** offer.

Finally, if you are happy with your range and level of skill, it might be worth undertaking specific training in making good job applications. Your local jobclub can help you here. Contact the Jobcentre for more information.

Training and Enterprise Councils

Every area has its own Training and Enterprise Council (TEC). In

Scotland they are known as Local Enterprise Companies (LECs). They are responsible for ensuring that work-related training in each area is relevant to local need and that there is an appropriate level and quality of training on offer. TECs and LECs devote considerable effort to liaising with colleges, local business organisations and training providers so they have a good grasp of the local scene.

In particular, they should be able to offer information on **Youth Training** opportunities, adult training opportunities, and business and enterprise training. Your local TEC may also be able to direct you towards retraining schemes for the long-term unemployed and updating courses for women returners linked to schemes which offer an allowance for childcare. Local colleges and employers are usually represented on management committees so the activities of each TEC should have a high level of local relevance.

Many TECs have local names and so it isn't always easy to find them in the telephone book unless you know what you are looking for. If you experience any difficulty in making contact, your town or county hall should be able to help you. Alternatively, ask your local education authority, the careers office or Jobcentre, the library or your local college of further education.

Transferable skills

Many jobs require remarkably similar skills. Each job demands a level of technical ability but, beyond that, the skills required in one job may be almost identical to those required in another. These skills are known as 'transferable' skills: you learn them as you move from job to job and they are always valuable no matter what job you do. When you are trying to get a job, think about the similarities between the job you are hoping to get and the jobs you have already done. What skills did previous jobs require? Are any of these skills required in the new job?

Have you, for example, developed a good telephone manner and are you able to take messages accurately and ensure that they reach the right person? Can you drive or use a keyboard? In the new job, will you be required to manage staff or deal with customers? Will you have to handle difficult situations, negotiate agreements, or account for money or stock? Will you be required to make presentations or write reports? If you have done any of these things previously, you should have few problems in applying them to your new situation. Different companies may have different styles and approaches but your transferable skills should give you a head start.

Transferable skills aren't necessarily learned or practised solely in the workplace. You may have developed a strong organisational ability through voluntary, charitable or sporting activities. It doesn't matter where or how you developed them as long as you recognise your strengths and make sure that potential employers are aware of them too.

When you apply for a job, look carefully at the job description and try to visualise the day-to-day reality of the job. Break down the responsibilities into a list of tasks and try to identify which skills will be required to handle each task. According to a job description, for example, the successful candidate may be 'responsible for arranging regular meetings between management and union officials, minuting meetings, and producing resulting reports and action plans'. Anyone tackling a job such as that would certainly need some organisational ability, some skill with people, and an ability to write reports, memos and minutes, as well as tact and discretion. All these skills could have been learned previously – transferred from another workplace or gained elsewhere.

List your transferable skills and you'll be pleasantly surprised by your range of abilities. For each skill you list, think of evidence you could offer to support your claim to be skilled in that area. Think of incidents which you have handled and tasks you have successfully completed in your life so far. Think also of pieces of work which you particularly enjoyed and try to analyse why they were so satisfying. What skills were required of you? Transferable skills are often overlooked in favour of technical knowledge, but they are equally important and you owe it to yourself to ensure that they are recognised.

Transport

When you are considering applying for a job, think about the transport arrangements you may need to make and the costs which you will incur. Distant jobs may pay more but the cost of transport may make a local job more attractive.

A car, motorbike or even a pedal cycle can sometimes be of great benefit, especially where shiftwork is involved. If you can get yourself to a 6 am to 2 pm shift, before the buses start running, or if you can provide your own transport in order to work in a 24-hour motorway service station, you have a distinct advantage over many other jobseekers.

Typing

Typing skill is still much in demand. If you can type, you can use a keyboard, and if you have keyboard skills, it is a simple matter to learn how to use a computer and a wide range of word-processing and computing systems.

Learning to use a computer keyboard is much easier than learning to master a typewriter. If you make a mistake on a word processor you can correct your work before printing it so accuracy is no longer as important as it was. Many word processors offer alternative spellings for words and suggest grammatical changes if you ask them to.

A word processor is a remarkably easy instrument to learn. Local colleges usually have a range of courses arranged on a full-time, part-time, evening or even a drop-in basis using teach yourself material. College tutors will be able to suggest appropriate courses. After a couple of lessons you'll never want to go back to a typewriter again. See also **Computer literacy**

U

Unemployed

This term is used to describe someone out of paid employment who is seeking a job. It is an unfortunate term, however, because people are natural workers. Even when out of paid employment they usually find some activity to occupy their time – decorating the house, gardening, or voluntary work of some description. Few people are content to sit around without an activity to employ them.

If you are committed to finding a job your days will be filled with purposeful activity and you'll be 'fully employed' in your efforts to find work.

V

Value-added

Recruiting new staff is never an easy process for employers. There are often many more applications than they would wish for and it can be difficult to reduce a pile of 30 or 40 letters and application forms to five or six candidates who seem worth looking at more closely. There are various techniques for arriving at a shortlist but, in many cases, the process results in the identification of several candidates who, on paper at least, could easily do the job detailed in the job description.

From an employer's point of view, it is possible that after the interview he may be faced with having to make a choice from among five candidates who all meet the requirements of the job. At this stage, he is in the enviable position of being able to look for a little more than he had originally planned. Now he can begin to look for the 'value-added' candidate – the one who has something to offer which is additional to the required mix of skill, experience, background and temperament.

One candidate may stand out from the rest because it is clear that he has the potential to grow beyond this job and take on more responsible positions in the company at a later stage. Another candidate may have developed skills elsewhere which are not required in this job but which may be needed in 12 or 18 months' time. Yet another may have had experience in working within a company as it underwent significant structural change. The ability to operate in uncertain times or the skill to progress during such changes may be an additional benefit which one particular candidate could offer over and above the job's requirements.

If you are invited to attend an interview, list the skills and qualities which you have over and above those required by the job description. Think about the added value that an employer would gain through offering you the job rather than anyone else.

Look beyond the job for a moment and try to get a view of what the company does and where it is going

- What can you contribute towards the general development of the organisation?
- Have you had experience of more modern equipment or a wider range of technology than this company uses at present?
- Do you have skills in more than one area?
- If someone from a different department was absent could you fill the gap for a while?
- Are you aware of the problems this company is faced with?
- Have you seen how they were successfully dealt with elsewhere?
- Do you have any skills or qualifications which are not essential to this particular job but may be useful to this company?

Having made a list of your value-added qualities you can now rehearse answers to questions which could arise at interview, making sure that your answers let the questioner know of the additional benefits you could bring to his organisation.

Voluntary Service Overseas

VSO was established in 1958 to support human development through working to improve people's education, health, income and employment opportunities, and their ability to contribute to society. To date, they have sent volunteers to work in nearly 50 countries in Asia, Africa, the Pacific and the Caribbean.

VSO is seen as a two-way process. By sending volunteers to work in developing countries they hope to have a direct effect on the quality of life in the communities they serve but they also see the experience as a learning event for the volunteers. On their return it is hoped that they will be able to promote international understanding by being better informed about how people live overseas and the factors which shape their lives.

As a VSO volunteer you will need to be willing to share your skills, pass on what you have learned in your education and working life, and be happy to learn new methods from your colleagues. You will also need to have patience, tolerance and an open mind so that you can adapt to life in another society where many things will be different and unfamiliar.

VSO volunteers sign up for two years and most find their overseas experience deeply rewarding. Candidates require some kind of professional or craft qualification and, in most cases, over 18 months' experience in the fields of education, health, technical trades and engineering, social development, business and commercial development, and natural resources. Applications are welcome from all people irrespective of their sex, race or creed. VSO also welcomes applications from disabled people. You can apply to join VSO at any age from 20 to 70.

If your application is accepted, you will be eligible to receive grants towards essential clothing and travel but while you are on location you will be paid a local wage, roughly the same amount as someone who does the job in that country on a permanent basis.

A recent survey carried out on 1100 returning volunteers shows that most who had hoped to return to their previous professions did so. Half the respondents who came home wanting to do something completely different managed to achieve this, as did the volunteers who had hoped to go on to further or higher education. The survey also showed that it took returning volunteers an average of just over two and a half months to find full-time employment back in the UK. Many who completed the questionnaire stated that VSO had helped them to find work on their return home. You won't get rich on VSO but the experience will be challenging, fulfilling and rewarding. You'll carry it with you for the rest of your life and you'll probably never be short of experiences to illustrate your strength of character at interview.

Further information
Voluntary Service Overseas, 317 Putney Bridge Road, London SW15 2PN; 0181-780 1331

Voluntary work

A paid job gives you a sense of identity, a feeling of worth, and a certain status in the community based on the fact that you are doing something worthwhile. If you are in work, you have a routine and a structure to your life. You also have a circle of friends and colleagues who keep you abreast of changes and developments. The wages you earn give you a degree of economic freedom and independence.

Listed above are seven good reasons for getting a paid job. If you are out of work, however, you can enjoy most of them by undertaking voluntary work. Being out of work when you don't want to be can be a painful experience. Unemployment threatens many aspects of your life and often the financial problems pale into insignificance against the loss of identity and self-respect, the feelings of hopelessness, marginalisation and depression, and the threat to health which many people face as a result of being out of work.

If you find being out of work a painful experience, a spot of temporary voluntary work can help you through the difficulties. Many people think of voluntary work as taking round the hospital trolley or delivering meals on wheels but this is a narrow view of what is available. All kinds of skill are required or can be learned through voluntary work. Some volunteers sell goods in charity shops, others carry out simple nursing duties. Some people keep accounts or become involved in publicising fund-raising events, teaching, counselling or organising activities.

Britain is very community-minded and no matter where you live there will be a range of local voluntary organisations which will welcome you and benefit from your efforts. Some organisations are charitable, others are educational, religious or even political. Some are local self-help groups, established to support people with particular needs or viewpoints, while others are local branches of nationally recognised organisations.

Each has its own particular aims and strategies but, from your point of view at least, they have common features. Almost all rely on the voluntary efforts of a wide range of people. They welcome interest and offers of help. Most are eager to put your skills to good use and, while they will not be able to pay you, they may be able to cover your expenses. Some organisations can provide training in new skill areas.

Undertaking voluntary work for an organisation which you happen to believe in can ensure that you retain your sense of identity, your self-respect and a feeling of worth. You can even enhance your reputation within your community and gain a great deal of satisfaction from the process. Voluntary work keeps you in the working framework. It holds you to a routine and ensures that you have a purpose and sense of direction. At interview, many employers ask how you have spent your time while being out of work. There is no better answer than to say that you have been undertaking voluntary work for a local organisation.

For some people, a period of voluntary work, undertaken while out of paid employment, has been a turning point in their lives. Parents of young children have often turned their backs on the commercial world after having enjoyed a period of voluntary work in their children's primary schools. Mature students on youth and community work training courses often report that their interest in and commitment to such work arose out of their voluntary efforts while unemployed.

Lists of local voluntary organisations and local branches of national voluntary organisations are kept in public libraries.

W

Word of mouth

Equal opportunity employers frown on the practice of advertising jobs only by word of mouth. They argue that a job which has not been advertised appropriately cannot fulfil equal opportunity requirements. How can you have an equal chance of getting a job if you didn't know the vacancy existed?

Despite these reservations, however, many employers still rely on word of mouth to recruit their staff. When you are looking for a job, don't ignore this. Let everyone know that you are seeking employment and ask them to tell you if they hear of a vacancy. You could find yourself a new job on a friend's recommendation.

Work experience

Most schools and many colleges offer students the opportunity of two or three weeks' work experience. If you have the chance, seize the opportunity with both hands.

Work experience allows you to see why the subjects you are studying are important and it can encourage you to put more effort into getting the grades and qualifications you need. It can also be a welcome and refreshing break from school or college, and it gives you a chance to test your ideas about particular jobs before you have to make a full commitment. Work experience teaches much more about a job than any textbook can and, if you are sure that this is the career for you, it can put you in touch with people in the business who may be able to offer you permanent work when you qualify. Some young people on work experience manage to create such a good impression that they are offered a job on the spot. Sandwich courses offered by some colleges of further education and higher education institutions are particularly good in this respect. By alternating study with regular work placement, you can make practical use of the theoretical knowledge you gain in the classroom while widening your range of contacts and broadening your workplace experience.

Young people don't have long histories of employment but a successful work-experience placement can add weight to a **curriculum vitae** and a good **reference** from the manager of the company in which you were placed can be valuable, especially if it complements an equally good reference from your school or college tutor.

Most participants enjoy their work-experience placement, but even if you don't you will probably learn something valuable. A few years ago one school student was convinced that hairdressing was the career for her until she tried out the job through work experience. After three weeks she discovered that she hated it. 'I couldn't stand it', she said. When asked why, she said that she had not realised from the textbooks how hard it is to stand all day bent over someone's head. 'I had aches and pains in every part of my body.' Better to learn now rather than three months into a college course.

Working abroad

If you have a professional qualification it can be easy to find work overseas. There are magazines and journals for nurses, teachers, engineers and technicians in which overseas jobs are frequently advertised.

Even without such a qualification it may be possible to secure work abroad before leaving this country by approaching holiday companies and camping firms, au pair agencies, or any of a large number of organisations which specialise in recruiting volunteers willing to work abroad for pocket money or expenses.

Finding work abroad is probably easier than you think. No matter whether you are looking for a job in London, Paris, New York or Tokyo, the same general principles apply. Energy, commitment and careful planning are the keys to success. Within the European Union all citizens have equal employment status. There are no work permits and you can move freely across frontiers in your search for employment. But elsewhere there may be a number of hoops to jump through before you leave this country. Consulates and embassies should be able to help you here.

If you have an adventurous frame of mind and are prepared to take a risk it is possible to travel and pick up work *en route*. If you don't speak the language, it is a good idea to spend some time before you go picking up a skill or specialism which transcends international frontiers – a qualification in teaching English as a foreign language, for example.

If you speak the language, bar jobs or jobs in hotels and restaurants shouldn't be difficult to obtain but the pay is usually poor. You can often do better if you have a recognised skill like a ski instructor's certificate or a canoeing or sailing qualification. Competition for these seasonal jobs is fierce but if you are there on the spot when the demand arises you could do well.

If you have some language skill, try to think of areas of employment where your ability to speak English could be of use – international car-hire firms, duty-free shops in ports and airports, or companies with strong British or US connections.

When thinking of working abroad, begin your planning and preparation as early as possible. Think about the country you are hoping to settle in and make a list of the things you need to consider:

- Will you need a visa?
- Will you need a work permit or permission to stay there?
- What about injections and inoculations?
- What realistic job opportunities are there for you?
- Is it an expensive country to live in?
- Will you be welcome there?
- Is it politically stable?
- How long do you intend to spend there?

Think about yourself and your strengths and weaknesses. Think also of the opportunities for employment in your chosen country and the threats to your chances of obtaining work there. How does it look? Is getting a job in this country a realistic proposition for you?

Finally, set about your careful preparation. Take on extra work or increase your overtime to get some money behind you, take language classes, try to develop a useful skill and do your research thoroughly. Many language schools, for example, recruit staff each September. You could be unemployed for several months if you arrive looking for this kind of work in June. Often, you need to get a fixed address in a country before you can get a job. Employers cannot contact you if you are moving from hotel to hotel. Before you leave try to set up appointments with possible employers and have your **curriculum vitae** and a standard **speculative enquiry** letter printed in the local language. Then establish a game plan. In many respects, once you arrive, getting a job in a foreign country is just like getting one at home. Establish a routine, use the directories, and visit every place where there is a possibility of employment. The first job you get may not be very good but it's a foot in the door. It will provide you with a base and give you time to develop your skills in the language. Working abroad is an adventure; no one said it would be easy.

Further information
Overseas Jobs Express, Premier House, Shoreham Airport, Shoreham by Sea, West Sussex BN43 5FF; 01273 440220. This is a useful monthly publication for professionals thinking of working abroad.

Vacation Work, Oxford, publish the following titles in their Live and Work in series: *France*; *Germany*; *Italy*; *Spain and Portugal*; *Belgium, Netherlands and Luxembourg*; *The USA and Canada*; *Australia and New Zealand*; and *Scandinavia* are due early in 1995.

Working for free

Don't dismiss the idea! There are times when it can be the best strategy. A period of unpaid work within a company can enable you to gain experience of a career area or a particular technique of which you have little or no knowledge. It can also be useful as a means of testing your suitability for a particular type of work before you embark on a period of training, and it can be a sound strategy for drawing your skills and qualities to an employer's attention. Many companies and highly experienced professionals undertake occasional unpaid work in order to obtain a prestigious reference or build on their network of contacts.

In teaching it is often expected that you will spend a couple of weeks in the classroom as a volunteer before embarking on a long course of teacher training. Candidates wishing to train as social workers are also usually expected to have gained an insight into the work through voluntary effort before they are accepted on a professional training course. Whatever type of work you are contemplating, it might be worth trying to spend a couple of weeks in an organisation before taking the plunge. Identify the type of work you wish to undertake and then think of the companies which seem to be the best known in that field. Give them a call or write to them. Mention your interest in the work and explain that you would like to widen your experience. Ask if you could make an appointment to discuss the idea of working voluntarily for them.

Working from home

For several years 'experts' have been predicting a revolutionary increase in the number of people who will work at home. They argue that fax machines, on-line computers and the development of the information superhighway will enable many of us to carry out most of our current job tasks from the comfort of our own homes. More recently, these experts have been moderating their views on the subject and today many now believe that the earlier predictions were optimistic in terms of the speed of the revolution and the number of people who will take up this **teleworking** way of life.

The possibility of working from home, however, isn't an option available only to secretaries and bookkeepers. Many self-employed people, in the early days at least, use their homes as a business base. Others, with ageing relatives or children to care for, have little choice but to explore the possibilities which working from home can offer. Some teachers, for example, use their homes to offer private tuition and coaching to examination entrants. Music teachers, in particular, often prefer to work from a home-based studio. A large number of health workers establish consulting rooms in their own houses, and many parents of young children supplement their income by becoming registered childminders.

But it isn't only the self-employed who are able to work from home. Some companies rely on large numbers of home-workers to undertake particular tasks for them – sending out mailshots, labelling envelopes, compiling statistics or other information from surveys, or generating business through direct telephone sales. Some companies even employ home-workers in aspects of the manufacturing process. Goods or raw materials are regularly delivered to each 'outworker' from the factory and then collected and returned to the factory for finishing at a pre-arranged time. Each worker has a quota and a deadline to meet and is paid accordingly.

Home-working has many attractions but there are some pitfalls for the unwary. Don't think of home-working as an escape from the rough and tumble of the outside world. As a home-worker, you still have bosses and customers to please and deadlines to meet. When you work from home, the pressures can be more intense – not less. As a home-worker, you cannot drop everything and go home – you're already there! Be careful too to make sure that your work doesn't take over the entire house. You need space and time for yourself, so you need to be able to put your work away and enjoy the wider aspects of your life from time to time. Most important, as a home-worker you will need to be highly motivated and disciplined. At home you set the times for work and you determine the pace. But home is full of distractions; you can stop for coffee whenever you want, pop out to the shops, or spend an extra 15 or 20 minutes watching the lunchtime soap; and if you don't make your quota you have only yourself to blame.

As a home-worker you can request an income tax allowance for the use of your home in the course of your business, but check out first that there is nothing in your deeds or tenancy agreement which prevents you from earning your living or operating a business from your home address. You may also need to check the views of your local council about the activity you intend to engage in. If you do decide to make an income tax claim, it should be based on an appropriate and reasonable portion of the total cost of the heating, lighting, cleaning and maintenance of your property, just as if you were claiming tax relief on the expense of running an office. Keep your claim 'general', however, and try not to claim for the exclusive use of any particular part of your house or flat for business purposes. If you identify a specific area of your home as business premises, you may find that you are building up capital gains problems for the future.

If you are seriously thinking about taking up a home-working job, check it out just like any other employment. Look at the rates of pay and the speed with which you will be expected to operate. Try to calculate the costs of home-working – extra heating and power, telephone charges, etc., and set these expenses against the income you feel you can generate. If it is the self-employment aspect of home-working which attracts you, all the usual advice on **self-employment** applies here.

X-ray yourself

Take a long, hard look at yourself and get to know yourself well because that's what an interviewer will try to do. He'll want to explore many different aspects of your personality and background and he'll ask questions to probe those depths of your character which he doesn't yet know. It helps if you've been there before him and prepared the ground.

- Why do you want this job?
- What aspects of the job will give you pleasure and satisfaction?
- How do you know that this is the job for you?
- How do you handle conflict?
- Is it important that you are liked by people and colleagues?
- How do you handle stress?
- How do you balance work and family commitments?
- What kind of things in the workplace could cause you sleepless nights?
- What would you hope to achieve within the first six months of getting this job?
- How would you measure your success?

As you consider these questions try to think of evidence to support your answers. What projects have you undertaken recently in or out of work? What examples can you give to show that you are enthusiastic, committed and willing to tackle new challenges? Turning the X-ray on yourself is a valuable exercise in preparation for an interview.

Youth Training

If you are young and the thought of staying on at school is too much to bear, think seriously about Youth Training. In theory at least, you are guaranteed a place if you are under 18 and not in a job or education. There is some evidence to suggest that in some areas the government has struggled to keep its promise on this but don't let that put you off. You can discuss the areas of work that interest you with careers officers or teachers and they will be able to advise you about the range of training placements available in your area. On Youth Training at 17 you can expect to be paid at least £35 per week, and although this isn't a fantastic wage, you will receive training to **National Vocational Qualification** standards in most cases.

When you are in the workplace you have a chance of turning your training placement into a real job. You will probably also meet other employers and get to hear of possible vacancies before they are advertised. Youth Training allows you to show an employer how good you can be and the qualifications you gain will support your claim to be competent and effective. Youth Training has plenty of critics but don't dismiss the idea until you have checked it out for yourself.

Z

Zest

What does the word mean to you? Freshness? Sparkle? Enthusiasm?
A sort of keenness perhaps? Any of these qualities will go a long way
towards impressing an employer. A crisp white shirt, newly washed
hair, good manners and an open smile all go a long way to impressing
an interviewer. They indicate that you have that freshness and sparkle
that he is looking for. A few well-chosen and prepared questions for the
end of the interview, and an eagerness to look over the premises if the
opportunity is offered, should convince him that you have enthusiasm
and the potential to become a first-rate employee.

The Kogan Page Careers Series

The series consists of short guides (96–114 pages) to different careers for school and college leavers, graduates and anyone wanting to start anew. Each book serves as an introduction to a particular career and to jobs available within that field, including details of training qualifications and courses. The following 'Careers in' titles are available in paperback. Enquiries phone 0171-278 0433.

Accountancy (*5th edition*)
Architecture (*3rd edition*)
Art and Design (*6th edition*)
Banking and Finance
  (*4th edition*)
Catering and Hotel Management
  (*4th edition*)
Environmental Conservation
  (*5th edition*)
Fashion (*3rd edition*)
Film and Video (*4th edition*)
Hairdressing and Beauty
  Therapy (*6th edition*)
Journalism (*6th edition*)
The Law (*6th edition*)
Marketing, Advertising and
  Public Relations (*5th edition*)
Medicine, Dentistry and
Mental Health (*6th edition*)

Nursing and Related Professions
  (*6th edition*)
Police Force (*4th edition*)
Publishing and Bookselling
  (*2nd edition*)
Retailing (*4th edition*)
Secretarial and Office Work
  (*6th edition*)
Social Work (*5th edition*)
Sport (*5th edition*)
Teaching (*5th edition*)
Television and Radio (*5th edition*)
The Theatre (*4th edition*)
Travel Industry (*4th edition*)
Using Languages (*6th edition*)
Working Outdoors (*5th edition*)
Working with Animals
  (*6th edition*)
Working with Children and
  Young People (*6th edition*)